Golden Handcuffs Review

Golden Handcuffs Review Publications

Seattle, Washington

Golden Handcuffs Review
Publications

Editor

Lou Rowan

Contributing Editors

Andrea Augé
Stacey Levine
Rick Moody
Toby Olson
Jerome Rothenberg
Scott Thurston
Carol Watts

Guiding Intelligence

David Antin

LAYOUT MANAGEMENT BY PURE ENERGY PUBLISHING, SEATTLE
WWW.PUREENERGYPUB.COM

<u>Libraries</u>: *this is Volume II, #24.*

Information about subscriptions, donations, advertising at:
www.goldenhandcuffsreview.com

Or write to: Editor, Golden Handcuffs Review Publications
1825 NE 58th Street, Seattle, WA 98105-2440

Contents

FICTION

MEMOIR

TRANSLATION AND TRANSFORMATION

RESPONSE

REVIEWS

"The Mysteries of Mind Laid Bare in Talking"

for David Antin (1932-2016)

Jerome Rothenberg

1
I would also say it
speaking   would like to hear it
catapulting from my mouth

not like a flow of words
but a barrage of pulses
one athwart the other

mindful how some spirit
wracked you
who were singular in speech

the mysteries of mind
laid bare in talking
discovered first, then lost

the way all times
are lost   when no one
counts them off

a dream expresses it
still harder to remember
pressured to write it down

they wait a new device
a camera to record
the images in dreams

the images in memory
of days in New York
or of walks in Paris

linked in talk
& warm embraces
on the other coast

is where we come
to die   at last
the more we wander

conversant with the dead
companions all
stiff necked & lonely

when you ask me for
a discourse
still more satisfying

that our cheating hearts
hold back
then let it fly

2
the memories
of being young
your black hair
in the wind

later to be lost
like *something*
keys hair someone
a contingency

my noble forehead
that you saw
or claimed to
in the loss of yours

the stream of language
hard to fix
or to deflect
once lost

first meetings
faces also lost
like words on paper
that we shared

carried over time
the thoughts
of sickness
shared with all

like dying
thrice denied
the distance between
now & now

I do not see you
any longer
but know the voice
full in my mind

so much like mine
someone had said
imagination all
that makes it sound

timed to my heart
that keeps the beat
flesh sundered
turned to ash

imagination
only
can it be fair
to write

a love song
to a friend

3
from friend to friend
the voice comes
& the answer
that a stranger overhears
robs him of speech

the guest is half
oracular
nowhere he turns
or runs   caught
in a web

or caught between
two open doors
is right for him
the way out west
leads back to asia

asia leads him
into wilderness
a bitter landscape
where no friend
survives

no gaze or touch
so tender
those who fight
for love
once living

know it as a taste
sweet in the mouth
though distant
at length   at last
the friend is double

in your sight
but turns from you
the time to come
draws nigh
then shatters

& does the poem exist
when there is no one there
to hear it?

4
who does not dream
dreams deeper
by not dreaming

until the door
swings open
draws you to
sleep within

what forms
assailing us
the scattered dreamers

curtains closing
on our eyes

in frantic bursts
lights streaming

take the shape
of birds & stars
outlyers

move across the sky
the eye in love
with tentacles
in mauve & amber

the new year
underway
without you

then the rest
is dream
whether the images
arise or not

the screen goes blank
foretold by you
the dreamer

here is the death
we feared
infinite space
to every side

absent all light

5

AFTER WANG WEI

O my friends! there is no friend.

at Weiching
        morning rain
                the fine dust damped
a guest house
        green among
                green willows
urge a friend
        to drink a final
                glass of wine
west of Yang Pass
        there is
                no friend

6

except the memory
the loss   a dream
that will not stick
but comes & goes
as if we hadn't
dreamed it

for which I name you
poet of the dream
in whose denial
dreams come forth
the word "desire"
foremost

pleasures first
a place as large
as Prospect Park
where others
feast & bathe
some sleeping

& the dreamer
kicks his shoes off
wades into a pool
the north branch of
an old estate
its master far away

then goes from room
to room in search
of shoes as prelude
to a silent movie
buried like his life
too deep for tears

for which the word
the woman
throws at him
is *hog* (he says)
not out of shame
or fecklessness

but turning
subject into object
echoing the master's
words   *the world*
is everything
that is the case

waking & dreaming
much the same

1.ii.2017

[N.B. The dream covered lightly in the final section, above, is from David Antin's "On Narrative: The Beggar and the King," published previously (2010) in Poems and Poetics (*Jacket2*).]

David Antin—thinking aloud

Rachel Blau DuPlessis

DAVID ANTIN IS OUR MONTAIGNE. His cultural work is remarkable. Basically he creates and sustains an informed but home-built philosophical cast of mind—witty, pensive, and ethical—from stories that look wandering but end up being exemplary. Exemplary that is, both in findings and in the didactic and pleasurable experiences of meandering in which you have participated with him. His philosophical zones are mainly ethics and aesthetics, but others as well. Epistemology. Ontology. Phenomenology. All those fancy names. What do I know. *Que sais-je?* But it is true. It's a "poetry" of thinking.

The talk-poems also have an existential flair—confronting responsibility, accepting consequences, making choices. He often discusses small acts with big implications. (Small—going shopping with his semi-cooperative aging mother, who is his opposite, it turns out, with a whole lifetime of avoiding anything that has "problems or interest" [*John Cage Uncaged is still cagey.* San Diego: Singing Horse Press, 2005, 68]). The work deliberates life, in all its intentional, half-baked, semi-connected, and curious acts, in fact, its acts of curiosity. The talk-poems are dramatic in their performative rhythms and pacing, but not—one might say never—stage-y or narcissistic. He proposes himself as an instrument of curiosity, wonder, and perception in the world, not performance as a display of his ego.

Antin weaves whatever is happening, what has happened, what might be happening, the likely, the unlikely and the naturalized quotidian, bringing temporalities and events together with a social ethnography in language, The improvisation is thoroughly casual, a working out right in front of you without particular defined beginning, and seemingly generating an eccentric "shaggy dog" story, deceptively teetering on the brink of losing its own thread. Antin is a shaman without a sacred mystique, but seeking rather the discursive flicker of recognition and fellow feelings. Like Robert Creeley, Antin is a master of stances and adjustments, moving around a topic, staging his own attentiveness in and as language choices.

So "Nu, voss is de sof" (what's the point) is a big question marked in his poetics. (*A Conversation with David Antin*, Antin and Charles Bernstein. NY: Granary Books, 2002, 12) This pert phrase declares that the work is about "it." Despite the many genial set-ups of the works that narrate his life (and sometimes Ellie Antin's and lives of friends and relatives), the work is never about "I" or for the gratification of "I," but about "it" and for the understanding of networks of "it."

Stories had "consequentiality and meaning."—Antin compares his personal talk poems to Jewish storytelling in Yiddish-speaking circles. "the people I grew up with told stories almost all the time," and these stories presented "arguments, in which [the stories] functioned as examples, evidence and counter evidence, testimony, mostly from experience" but also possibly from newspaper or dreamed...functioning "as models, metaphors, parables, or as paradoxes, as jokes...." (*A Conversation*, 12) Another writer who inherited this whole skeptical, humane and comic Yiddish tradition of the refreshing outside look, the skeptical-joyous naif is Grace Paley.

Like Paley, David Antin works in a post-popular-front tradition of human meaning and ethics, tracking the location and imbedding of ourselves in contingent social relations. These are texts of exemplification. One story leads to another via a deeply buried question or intransigent underground dilemma, somehow ending simultaneously in the implacable and optimistic. Any conclusion or idea is often delivered sideways, by inference or listener extrapolation. In this he is similar as well to a writer whom he knew and had observed: George Oppen. His memoir of Oppen in *The Oppens Remembered : Poetry, Politics, and Friendship* is like a channeling of Oppen's own oblique stories, precisely understated and focused by inferential subtlety (ed. DuPlessis, Albuquerque: University of New Mexico Press, 2015).

In the talk poems, everything is happening on the same lively, horizontal level, even in the most stunning questions, in culminating questions like "who is speaking when I speak," and other such dilemmas. So too, Antin has rendered the talk-poems' linked anecdotes in an apparently unprioritized manner at first quirkily annoying, visually raggedy, and then clearly based upon a choice of rhetorical ethics. "ive tried to distinguish them from printed prose by dispensing with its nonfunctional markers   regular capitalization most punctuation marks and right and left   justification   which I see as merely marking propriety and making a   dubious claim to right thinking and right writing" (Preface, *I never knew what time it was*, U.C Press, 2005, x).

The work certainly gives an impression of being open-ended, open at both or all—ends. The pulse of spaces without periods indicates porosity: open to permanent questioning and rumination, Playful about the fact that life is going on and on—without particular thesis even if it is one's clear task to live by some values. But sometimes, in a striking counterturn against callow aesthetics of all kinds, there is indeed a moral and not simply the play of inference. In "What it means to be avant-garde" (in the 1993 book of that title), the rumination touches on oldness, aging and grief, presence and absence, connection and loss, life and death, people/relatives and the void. The revelation occurs in a phone call to his old aunt, in which he hears abruptly, of the unexpected death of his uncle, after which Antin delivers the scandalous punchline—"if you can't respond to this you're not in the avant garde." In which statement are precipitated many ethical and provocative points about what the avant-garde in fact is and of what values it is constituted—perhaps something like a position of emotional mobility and responsiveness to metamorphosis and fact and a humane comprehension of grief. Antin may have unstated beginnings to these works, but he mainly does not have unstated endings.

These are not prose poems—they are the opposite. Not "poetic," not invested in making an iconic and amusing object—no *amuse-bouches* in Antin. The history of Antin's doing this kind of work can be tracked in "A Few Words" (from 1963) at the beginning of his *Selected Poems 1963-73* (1991), as he stopped writing a novel and stopped writing an "image" [Deep Image] poetry that he found "more decorative than meaningful." The question of what genre he was trying to declare had to be quite bemusing and even painful when he was making the transition to talk-poems (apparently some time in the early 1970s with the statement "[My work] wasn't aiming at psychological depths which I didn't believe in. It was aiming at perfectly straightforward experience, which I did believe in." (Interview conducted by Barry Alpert in *VORT #7*, 1973). This pragmatic epistemology and "realist" aesthetic, Antin makes comically clear in one of the first works,"what am I doing here?" delivered at San Francisco State, in 1973. One of the most famous of Antin's aphoristic pronouncements, for instance, is:

> if robert lowell is a
> poet I don't want to be a poet   if robert frost was a
> poet I don't want to be a poet   if socrates was a poet
> ill consider it

This declaration of allegiances--and, indeed, it is precisely this particularly in the context of famous poets of the 1960s—aims not so much to define what a poet is or should be (nor simply to call any such definition into question) as to bring the very act of thinking--as active and provocative Socratic discipline, directly into play as poetic *praxis*. Begin anywhere, Antin seems to say, work honestly and with an amused humility, and it will lead you where *you* most distinctively can go. Begin *in situ*, in a location, with some sense of listener/ interlocutors, and with a set of possible questions, an unpretentious bemusement, a bafflement that you are willing to test out publicly as if at a permanent crossroads of thinking.

Antin has rejected "poetry" or the construction of completed, iconic (and sometimes mannered) objects in favor of "poesis," the active ongoingness of making by thinking out connections, constructing structures of frank association and risk from tracking one's own essay-mind at work. He builds right in front of us, loop by loop, and brings us to exist in the saturated present of being, facing the dilemmas and paradoxes of Now. It's like seeing someone building Watts Towers loop by loop, minute by minute. His work has the drive, obsessive intensities and determination of Simon Rodia, or other of the more convincing outsider artists.

In his apparent casualness, Antin can be a devastating and amusing critic; in his wry improvs, he produces a genial shamanic flicker, not going for the sacred aura, but for the inquisitive ethnographic moment of curiosity and analysis. David Antin is a poet-philosopher of the contact zones among us, not only between and among us. but including our various multiples in dialogue inside our singular selves.

And then you realize his medium is secular human wisdom.

Elegy for David Antin

Hank Lazer

what to say
of one so bright
who now
is dead
who could talk
& talk
like no other
an intelligence
in so many
directions
talking like a
brooklyn tough
talking about
wittgenstein &
cage talking
in a way
that got under
people's skin
an irritation
that made you
think   hard

now to picture
that infinite
momentum
permanently
at rest
& who
will take it
up again
who
in his
or her
own way
will carry on
david's
talking
& tell
a new
web of
stories
with his
questions
& humor
& intelligence
electric as
any thinker
he ever
mentioned
who will
enter
the silence
of his
death
there where
the mind
might live
to say
what is
the present

10 / 14 / 16 Cambridge / Selwyn College

David Antin:
listening and listing[1]

Hélène Aji

or maybe i should go in with a video camera instead of a view

camera   and ask these people if they want to tell me what they

think its like   their life   and i shoot it and show it to them so

they can give me their second thoughts about it   because maybe

they think their first thoughts werent right   it seems to me

most people would want to take a crack at that   making their

own self-portrait   especially if they arent worried about their

lack of readiness or competence and have a chance for second thoughts

except perhaps in that part of the art world where no one has

second thoughts about his life   because you cant have second

thoughts where there are no first ones

(Antin "remembering recording representing" *in* Dawsey 190)

---

[1] The final version of this article owes a lot to the editing suggestions made by three students in my poetry seminar at the University of Texas at Austin (Fall 2017): Hailey Kriska, John Calvin Pierce, and Emma Whitworth were supportive and constructive as I struggled with the distressing fact of writing about David's work without David.

In "remembering recording representing," David Antin imagines a project to collect autobiographies that would kindly allow the autobiographers to have "second thoughts," and amend their first accounts. As an ironical afterthought, he adds a slightly cryptic twist: how can one have second thoughts "where there are no first ones"? This is much further reaching than at first sight, as with much of David Antin's work: in the context of the present article it translates into an invitation to reconsider the work, what has been said about it, and what may have remained largely unsaid because unthought in the first place. The striking form of the talk-poem and massive corpus that falls into this category could be seen as "second thought": the original actualization of a more overall procedural strategy that presides over Antin's poetic production from the beginning.

In his introduction to the *Selected Talk Poems of David Antin*, Stephen Fredman calls forth the key concepts that preside over any assessment of the work, and, with mentions of Marcel Duchamp, Allan Kaprow and Andy Warhol, outlines less of a lineage than a possible community of intention able to transfer the poet outside "the limits of poetry" into the domain of the visual arts, and of performance:

> Like the conceptual pioneers who eschewed technique but redefined the medium and contexts for visual art, such as Duchamp, Kaprow, and Warhol, Antin is an adventurous explorer assessing the limits of poetry. Giving up the attractive coloration of meter, rhyme, alliteration, assonance, and stanza form, his talk poems offer instead brilliant bursts of intellectual light provoked by radical demythologizing, linguistic playfulness, conceptual enigmas, new theoretical discoveries, and uncanny collisions among a company of memorable characters. (Fredman "Introduction" in Antin *Selected* xxiii)

The poetic medium is questioned, as its conventional defining traits are discarded, though one may find in Antin's texts alternative reinvestments of these traits, informing and structuring an only apparently continuous flow of discourse: meter is deprived of its fixity but still present on the page as spacing alludes to the persistence of feet; the unjustified margins make up lines that resist the temptation of prose; sounds and words return in rhythmic patterns; or the twists and turns of digression as demonstration form proto-stanzaic movements that lead from irruption to interruption, from the onset of the talk to its provisional closure. Myth, language, conceptualization, the exploratory qualities of speech, the challenges of contingency and contiguity are indeed the so-to-speak nuclear cores of Antin's work, radiating from all of his texts, from the early experiments of the *november exercises* to the more widely disseminated talk-poems.

As in the liminary quote from Antin, the preoccupations focus on some key issues: accounting for the reality of experience; evidencing the processes of memory and witnessing; adapting accounts to present situations; assessing the conditions for the production of this discourse about experience through iterated performance. Like the people in the fictitious video project of "remembering recording representing," the poet needs to overcome or at least control his doubts about the relevance of his "self-portrait," and his "worries" about being not "ready" or "competent" enough. The challenge rests in addressing Antin's work as a whole, beyond talking back to the talk-poem: we need to "take a crack at that" now, to borrow Antin's own colloquial expression. The variety of his procedural experimentation overflows the specificity of the talk-poem, and works up to it as a series of attempts, that have a cumulative effect in their iterations and variations. The talk-poem, in its written transcribed version from the recording of a performance, is "second thoughts". In the quotation above, lineation plays on the phrase, separating "second" from "thought" in the third instance of the terms: it is elusive "thought," postponed to the next line as it is postponed from experience.

Thinking as a provisional process is what the talk-poem evidences. The streamlined conditions of the poem's production show the heterogeneity of Antin's art rather than what is often described as a homogeneous idiosyncratic poetic form. The talk-poem implies a procedural process involving multimedia creation: live performance; audio recording; transcription into a single continuous text; inclusion into the "radical coherency" of a volume; integration into the massive diversity of an archive. It articulates what is at stake not only with his poetry but with poetry at large in a world that is "post" (postwar, post-Holocaust, postmodern...), and which this paper will try to address: the relation to reality or Antin as "debunker of the real"; the choice of audio and text over video as testing the delusion of presence in performance; the production of minor narratives as method to undermine the dictatorship of master narratives; the choice of procedural modes of composition to define the boundaries of the author's authority.

With "whos listening out there," Antin does not just raise the question of the work's reception (who these people in the audience are, what their expectations are, and how the mechanisms of "hearing" what they are listening to are activated, in their openness and limitations.) The anecdote told by Marjorie Perloff collapses the 1979 talk-poem with an event she had organized when Antin's practice collided with the expectations of a "listener":

> Here an anecdote may be apposite. In 1980 or so, I invited David to give a poetry reading—that is, a talk—at USC. The auditorium was reassuringly full. But about ten minutes into the piece—I think it was 'Who's Listening out There?'—David was interrupted by a woman's voice from the audience. 'When,' she asked impatiently, 'does the poetry reading begin?' Everyone laughed. 'You're not going to hear anything you're not hearing now,' David responded calmly, 'so feel free to leave. There is nothing else coming.' She stayed. (Perloff 179)

It is this article's contention that the succession of Antin's experiments with the poem as concept (the idea of composition), process (the modes of composition) and product (the resulting textual objects) generate a list of instances of listening to one man listening to the poem of contingency. Each of these instances stand as so many hopeful incitations to oneself and others towards a non-prescriptive, non-normative listening to the world.

"Debunker of the 'real'"

On second thoughts, then, if one returns to the "discrete series" of Antin's poems now housed in the Getty archive,[2] including all his texts published and unpublished, official in books or ensconced in the secrecy of notebooks, one might want also to reconsider Lita Hornick's 1979 chapbook, *David Antin Debunker of the "Real."* Although relatively thin, it is most certainly the first (and as yet only) book to be entirely devoted to his work: it is committed to the work and its evolutions in open admiration of Antin's audacity. A downside of this is that it remains consistently descriptive whereas it could have interrogated its own categories: both the "debunking" and the "real." Antin's demystifying and de-mythologizing processes do

[2] On this, see Perloff 178.

not so much cancel myth as they propose alternative constructions of myth and collective expression through the de-realization and conceptualization of personal reality. A recurrent dynamic of the talk-poem is thus to take over the material of individual experience and construct its convergence through contiguity with other seemingly disconnected events: a kind of common denominator emerges allowing the provisional formulation of an idea and thus bringing the poem to a close. This is the conclusion Stephen Fredman draws from Antin's poetic practice in his notes for the 1975 issue of *Vort* dedicated to both David Antin and Jerome Rothenberg:

> His method is what Lévi-Strauss (*The Savage Mind*) calls *bricolage*--a man pulls used elements out of his sack and throws them together so they make a structure that fits the present need. Lévi-Strauss sees this as homologous to myth-making. A scientist differs in that he invents new materials. An artist is between the two. Antin leans more toward pure *bricolage* in his Talkings. He tries to argue ideas with other poets & push them into his way of thinking--but that misses the point: it's not his way of thinking but his way structuring that is unique. (Fredman "Notes on Antin" *Vort* 66-67)

The extent to which Antin's talk-poems enforce structure (through Lévi-Straussian *bricolage* and structuralism) rather than de-center it and deconstruct it (as with Jacques Derrida's initial take on the epistemological limitations of any systematizing normative process[3]) can be discussed. David Antin himself carries out this discussion when he describes the awakening from the "dream" of Claude Lévi-Strauss to the transformation of the domain of hard science into an art domain.[4] The detour of myth and art leads to a redefinition of the "real" as other than reality. This "real" is what discourse deals with, since reality is nowhere to be found as soon as mediation occurs. This "real" emerges as an abstraction characterized by its relativity, and provisionality. So, what Hornick's book does in a ground-breaking albeit unassuming manner is to outline and problematize the transition between the procedural

---

[3] See "Structure, Sign and Play in the Discourse of the Human Sciences" (1970) in *Of Grammatology.*

[4] "It may be that Lévi-Strauss was suffering from modernist delusion when he imagined that anthropology would lie down among the social sciences to rise among the natural sciences. It may, after a troubled sleep, like linguistics, like sociology, like history, like psychology, or even mathematics, profitably wake up to find itself among the arts." (Antin "Postmodernism?" 134-135)

and ironic work of the beginnings (the *november exercices, the london march, novel poem* notably that are based on systematic appropriation and recontextualization of found text) and the stabilized idiosyncratic form of the "talk-poem," as first evidenced in "talking at pomona" (1972). The transition may seem to yield a new poetic genre, but it also represents one possibility to draw the formal consequences from a dynamic reflection on the "real," this experience of reality in the present and its interpretation in language.

In this perspective, Hornick indicates directions for further inquiry into Antin's poetics: the diverse forms of the poem, culminating with the talk-poem, emerge from an ongoing attention paid to the real as experienced reality. The malleability of the textual medium allied to the devising of specific modes of composition thus generates changeable formations and "configurations" (Hornick 7). She indeed spells out major lines of questioning that inform David Antin's work: about occasion and the occasional poem; about readiness, preparation, and the accomplishment of one's project; about dislocation in composition when one ceases to conform with the convention of "sitting at a typewriter and addressing a hypothetical audience" (16-17). Although she primarily seems to be limiting herself to an introduction to David Antin, a relatively young and lesser known poet at the time, she in fact brings to the fore the ontological issues that are consistently addressed by the poet. The evolving tactics of the poem try to circumscribe these questions, at the same time as they evidence their pervasive and irredeemably "enigmatic" qualities (Fredman "Introduction" in Antin *Selected* xxiii).

> His major theme is the ambiguity of truth in all human learning and all mental configurations. Related to this are the themes of the ambiguity of the self and the unreliability of memory. (Hornick 7)

Test of presence

"Ambiguity," and "unreliability," these are not so much "themes" of the poems as what the poems come to embody: they enact the instability of knowledge and understanding at every level. They engulf in a common condition of mutability the producer of the text, the processes of its production, a product that is objectified in multiple media, and a whole gamut of potential receivers. The audiences of the poems range from the witnesses

of the performance to the hypothetical readers of a book, through
the frustrated listeners of a tape who, like Barry Alpert in 1975, wish
they could see the source of the voice and who wonder about Antin's
refusal of video:

> The ontology of Antin's improvised oral poetry is unusual, to say
> the least. A talk first exists as it is being articulated live by David
> Antin. The original aural experience can be simulated by listening
> to a tape-recording of the talk proper. Since one can listen to any
> part or the whole talk any number of times, the audiotape is not
> merely a canned substitute for the original experience. It has an
> unfixed temporal existence of its own. Antin hasn't yet arranged,
> as far as I know, to have one of his improvised performances
> videotaped. Since he's worked with videotape before, I'm not
> clear about his reasons. The videotape would share certain
> possibilities inherent in the audiotape and at the same time
> compensate more adequately for the absence of Antin's human
> presence in the poem. (Alpert "Post-Modern Oral Poetry" 680)

Alpert's suggestion of video as "compensating" for Antin's absence
"more adequately" than audio expresses a deeply-ingrained
desire for and fantasy of an actual presence of the poet and the
poem. In better-known terms, this reader aspires to what William
Carlos Williams would qualify as an idolizing relationship both to
the poet and to his text: yet if we want "to cease to be idolators,"
says Williams, we must stop confusing reality and its "signs" (*The
Embodiment of Knowledge* 182).

This is why the audiotape is paradoxically successful thanks
to its very shortcomings: as can be experienced by listening to
the recordings from the Getty digital collections, audio subtracts
the body, foregrounds the absence of the poet, and intensifies
the efforts of attention to the text. In print, the poem is further
disembodied, but encounters a new materiality. The formatting
intervenes at that point to extend the reader's estrangement from
the poet as person through the deliberately bizarre and disorienting
typesetting of unjustified margins, lack of punctuation, phonological
word spacing and spelling. Consistently Antin's works signal how
his texts deal in the "signs" for experience rather than in the actual
experience. Formal exploration, in Alpert's evaluation, is directed
at an idealized total conservation of the "original aural experience,"
which he assumes would be better approximated with the use of
video than with audiotapes. But if one considers Antin's commitment

to oral poetry and, to some extent, to ethnopoetics from the 1960s onward and mainly through his awareness of his friend Jerome Rothenberg's work, this conservation may not be the objective of Antin's experiments with the form of the poem: rather it is what is lost in representations of the lived moment that is exhibited, both in the staging of memory in all the talk-poems and through the lacunae in the conservation process.

The dubious case for audio over video may be meaningful in the way absence is foregrounded by the explicit choice of partial traces against a medium that could provide the delusion of integral persistence of the original experience over time. Key to Antin's devices, radical ephemerality and incompleteness, loss of aura, of intensity and of information are built into the structure in ways that are not to be "compensated." As Alpert underlines, and Jill Dawsey reminds us, David Antin promoted video as a major art medium as early as 1971, but chooses not to use it himself. He "took a group of graduate students with him to learn video production in the only place on campus where that was possible: in the basement of the medical school, where autopsies were videotaped for teaching purposes" though (Dawsey "Introduction" 18). What was to be learnt about video production from the videotaping of autopsies at the medical school? Were those morbid occasions the only ones available for Antin's teaching of video to his visual arts students, or did the fact of these videos' objects (dead bodies to be dissected) provide an embedded reflexive comment on some lethal effect of video on its objects despite the assumption of a total, "live" recording?

Antin's take on video is that it might work only if used as a recording device that can be corrected (Antin "remembering recording representing" *in* Dawsey 190), and not as the answer to the wild fantasy of seizing the present and recovering life through aesthetic and poetic devices. Sherman Paul's appraisal of the task of the talk-poem, its objectives and achievements thus echoes Barry Alpert's wish for video:

> The talk poems restore the primacy of speech and demonstrate some of the things that enable us to live in a human universe. As the title of some of them tell us, there is the need to be (in the) present, in the here/now of one's occasion; to live one's life now and not, as Thoreau would say, postpone it. We are always in

> the right place; it is always the right time. And we can have our
> lives by contacting them, by talking about them. (Paul 42)

The poem as direct response to existential imperatives is not a
notion foreign to Antin's own practice of composition, as he redefines
the status of the poetic text by turning it, apparently at least, into
the raw transcription of a language event. This emerges as an
alternative take on earlier or contemporary destabilizations of the
text which, according to Antin himself, have stemmed from the vogue
of poetry readings. The poem as "score" (as in Jackson Mac Low)
or as "notation" (as in Charles Olson) "occupies a middle ground
between an idea of oral poem and an idea of literature" (Antin
"Modernism" 132). Yet, the poem as "in the present" or literature as
"of the present," which video might seem to support, are but decoys.
The "primacy of speech" claimed by Paul (42) cannot be sustained;
Antin's work stages the unavoidable "secondariness" of all discourse.
Video tries to obliterate the fact that life is lost in mediatization. It fails
in doing so, but does occasionally support delusions of presence
and immediacy. Significantly, the same tension between success
and failure informs Antin's discussion of modernism in *Occident* as
early as 1974, and feeds into the general debate over genre and
medium. "Art's claim to truth" (Antin "Some Questions" 37) persists
and motivates the redefinition of genre and medium as notions in
flux, rather than as fixed *loci* for the production of art:

> The point is that modernism to play itself out had to step away
> from the Romantic domain of definition in order to determine
> to what degree the application of the fundamental axiom for
> defining the medium was necessary and sufficient in itself.
> This resulted in a new version of the fundamental axiom: *it is
> necessary to define the medium of action, the elements that are
> acted upon and the operations that are performed upon them to
> make a work or a body of works.* The defining act had become
> a mechanism for generating work or, to use the somewhat more
> appropriate computer terminology, a program. Clearly this
> version of the axiom does not require distinctive uniqueness
> for the medium because the medium is not permanent. It is
> not "the medium" of art or of an art, it is "a medium"–that is a
> temporary arena, which may be used several times or once and
> be abandoned without regrets. (Antin "Some Questions" 37)

As a medium implying production and post-production, video
cannot be an arena of choice over audio, for instance, since the

stakes are in not in finding a single medium of choice but in using several choices of labile media. Rather than being exclusive of one another, these media remain in constant interaction. By editing and erasing the markers of discourse through montage, video suppresses heterogeneity and the signs of hybridization, doing to reality something akin to what, in Antin's words, "story" does to "narrative": video produces "corpses" that retain the appearance of life in the same way as stories piece together types of information to produce a homogeneous and continuous whole. Story homogenizes sources to the extent of canceling their tense inadequacies and of preventing the processes of their hybridization.[5] In the videos of autopsies of UCSD medical school, the interest lies not just in the technology but in the implications of this technology made explicit by their incidental objects: the fantasy of life conservation through the moving image is simultaneously staged and undermined, recorded and remembered against odds as one witnesses the *mise en abîme* of clinical dismemberment. The "fraud" is in the pseudonarrative or fiction of direct witnessing and presence which it enforces, in ways similar to what Antin calls the political "pseudonarratives" of history: processes that generates fake agents and fake facts which dogmatic discourses and ideologies instrumentalize to limit the range of individual or collective self-awareness.

> I think you have a narrative corpse or, to put it another way, you can have a fraudulently invented narrative, a pseudonarrative, as in political narratives. Historical narrative is often of this order. For example, master narratives of a nation's history are generally pseudonarratives undertaken for particular subject enjoyment, and they've tended to engender a justifiable distrust for narrative history among historical scholars. They become pseudonarratives when they begin to generate pseudosubjects like "the people," "the working class," "the revolutionary spirit,"

---

[5] Significantly Antin returns to the issue in many of his essays, and some of the talk-poems, attempting to address the persistence of these categories that prevent at the same time as they provoke experimentation and the rise of artistic avant-garde. See for instance his 1989 essay "The Stranger at the Door": "As many, and perhaps even more, of my contemporaries would be dissatisfied with it, apparently definition is no more useful for the notion of a genre than it is for the notion of a family. Seen from this view point the viability of a genre like the viability of a family is based on survival, and the indispensable property of a surviving family is a continuing ability to take in new members who bring fresh genetic material into the old reservoir. So the viability of a genre may depend fairly heavily on an avant-garde activity that has often been seen as threatening its very existence, but is more accurately seen as opening its present to its past and to its future." (Antin "Stranger" 245)

"the citizen," "France," "the Free World," which are usually
endowed with fictive feelings that suggest fantasy subjectivities.
(Antin *in* McHale 98)

"Minor" narrative?

Antin's narrative would then be "minor" in the sense given
to the term by Gilles Deleuze in his comments on Franz Kafka's
use of the German language in writing his fiction: the language is
made strange to itself through the more or less perceptible thwarting
of conventions. This strangeness questions narrative conventions
and their coercive implications.[6] Similarly, when Antin mentions
"master narratives," he refers to the danger of master narratives
pointed out in Jean-François Lyotard's comments on the postmodern
condition, an essay first published in French in 1979, and pervasively
commented upon by scholars at the same time as the most intense
phase of talk-poem production. Antin turns to the talk-poem not to
tell stories, but to practice stories until they are demystified. Narrative
"explains nothing," contrary to the explicitiness and cohesiveness
of "story." Rather narrative highlights "the struggle of the subject
to maintain his existence," and "is the shamanistic transmission of
the confrontation" (Antin *in* McHale 101). The dynamics at work in
the anecdote about buying socks for his mother at Sears is in this
respect emblematic: the poet departs from the anecdote to reassess
the coherencies (and incoherencies) at work in the world that
surrounds us. He also suggests possibilities to subvert them:

> and now whats beginning to interest me is that once
> there was a kind of coherency   a fully articulated
> system of hosiery that included waist height stockings
> and knee stockings and calf stockings and ankle
> stockings   and maybe also toe stockings
> but whatever the system contained   at this
> particular moment   all that is left of the system
> is whats on the shelves   and such logical
> structure as we can infer from whats left   and whats
> left turns out to be calf height   and my mother is
> once again getting depressed   so i grab three pairs
> of calf height stockings and assure her that she can
> cut them down to anklets when she gets them home
> (Antin "radical coherency" 186-187)

---

[6] On this see Deleuze on Kafka notably, in a text published in 1975.

The anecdotal story, because it is steeped in the personal, stops short of "master" status; the succession of such stories triggers a conceptual distance that allows narrative to show its stakes. Thus as contrasted with story, which structures, organizes, and imparts teleology, narrative refrains from the "defective" "logical structuring" Antin finds in Brechtian "alienation or estrangement technique" (Antin in McHale 107). The aporia resides in the necessity both of story and of narrative; the difficulty lies in the distinction between these intertwined notions: "you need the story to grasp the logical course of the change. But without the narrative you wouldn't have the sense of what was at stake" (Antin *in* McHale 101).

In the 2004 interview with Brian McHale, that targets poetic activity as "narrative" Antin gives the example of newspaper stories, and the way they "piece the story together" "into a more or less logical structure" (Antin *in* McHale 97). The example is a reponse to Kenneth Golsdmith's work, which David Antin knew very well. The newspaper takes front stage indeed in Goldsmith's 2003 publication of *Day*, the literal transcription of the September 1, 2001 issue of the *New York Times* from front to last pages: through different modes or methods, both Antin and Goldsmith aim at "inferring several possible subjectivities and several possible but unrepresented narratives" (Antin *in* McHale 97). Both Antin and Goldsmith play on the side effects of the expository modes of text. Through literal transcription of every line of the paper from beginning to end in strict succession, Goldsmith returns the different stories to the chaotic state of partial pieces of discourse to be patched together. Unredacted again, the stories cannot recover the integrity of the journalist's discourse since the reader cannot circulate within the issue to follow the story any longer. Dismantled once through the issue's composition, then a second time through transcription, the stories become reminders of their own instability and tenuous relationship to a truth of fact. In *Day*, no story will remain unread if one does read the book, but none will acquire the polished closure of what Antin calls "pseudonarrative"; similarly the successive stories in the talk-poem signal their temporary relevance and interchangeability.

With the talk-poem, the main mode which develops is based on successive reminders of "the transactions we undertake with one another," of our "effort to create a continuum which makes self possible" and how this process is "always conditioned by the nature of the person to whom you are relating" (Hornick 7). The encounter evidences less the "dialogical" dimension of the talk-poems evoked by Paul,[7] than the structural significance of "contiguity" mentioned by Hugh Kenner in his brief *Vort* piece:

> Contiguity is the oldest of encoding devices. Utterances emitted serially, utterances recorded in adjacent spaces, affirm some perception of connectedness. (Kenner "Antin, Cats, &c." *Vort* 85)

Kenner's comment bears essentially on the linguistic process at work within the talk-poem, through the succession of utterances that connect because they unfold in succession. This remark however goes beyond the observation of a language phenomenon. If the stories produce meaning through the very fact of their "contiguity," it is in this contiguity that intention is located, overcoming and perhaps belying their declared randomness (many Antin stories are incidents or accidents), or the suspicious serendipity of their relevance to the question at hand in the talk. In "The Price," for instance, the discrepancy between the successive stories helps emphasize the underlying questions raised by the poet about heroism.

> because every functionary knows the story of nathan hale
> and has an idea of what it might be like to look disdainfully
> over the redcoat bayonets and say "I only regret that i have
> only one life to give for my country"   even though they
> may despise both hale and his country and say to themselves i
> am not only not nathan hale but ive never wanted to be nathan
> hale and i dont admire nathan hale   what i want is a quiet
> life in the country or a condominium with a swimming pool and
> a jacuzzi   and anyone who wants anything else is stupid or
> a troublemaker
>
>
> but the knowledge that thats what you want and how
> much you want it and are willing to pay for it is also an
> organization of a subjectivity around the fault line of some
> potential narrative crisis   that might dry up your jacuzzi
>   (Antin *Selected Talk Poems* 352)

Such contiguity within the poem allows for the emergence of a whole range of meanings, at times contradictory: where Antin seems

---

[7] On this see Paul 21, and in particular: "The talk poems are also dialogical because, in Buber's sense, he meets us. Reality—perhaps the poems represent this reality too—reality, real living is meeting. The poems are relational events (Buber's phrase). As Dick Higgins, who was there, says of exemplative art, 'the action is always between'."

to attack heroism as self-sacrifice, he simultaneously shows the construction of subjectivity and its survival as conditioned by such heroic projections of the self. It is the thematic version of a contiguity that connects the successive versions of the work, and assert its transient nature.

The diverse incarnations of the work, in performance, on tape, in transcription, in reader reception, indeed underline the provisional dimension of art in Antin's practice, as well as they enforce a technical consistency, turning each so-called improvisation into a crafted piece. Through their plural contiguities, the talk-poems materialize the impossibility of integral conservation, the serial affirmation of ephemerality, and the poet's realization of any work's circumscribed relevance (to the occasion, to the circumstances of time and space, to the constitution of temporary and unstable communities). This circumscribed relevance is not a fault in the work but rather the very condition for its relevance.

Furthermore this relevance is not solely circumstantial in what Barrett Watten may call a "presentist" commitment (Watten 137ff): it is scripted, and encrypted into the overall production of the poem through a diversity of procedures. One of these procedures presides over the production of the talk-poem The talk-poem is not just what we find in, for instance, Antin's New Directions series of books: it is a total, intermedial and transitory object made of preparation in notation and score, participative production and reception in performance, transcription, edition, publication, reception in print. And still this enumeration might be lacking since the poetic aim to precipitate a crisis of art media is reactivated with each of the poet's interventions.

"Underlying procedure" (Antin in Conversation 46)

In this respect, David Antin's take on the "happening" acquires new resonance. In his descrition of Allan Kaprow's happenings, Antin focuses on the anticipation of the event in "script," and the constraint of "precise instructions" that may generate a "chaotic appearance," but remain orchestrated and organized:

> I didn't see happenings as chaotic. Almost every happening I saw or took part in was carefully scripted. There is certainly in the '60s work a kind of baroque painterly quality to surfaces. But Robert Whitman's work, Ken Dewey's, Allan Kaprow's work

in particular, were tightly scripted. Allan's performers usually received very precise instructions and had specific jobs to carry out. The chaotic appearance resulted from the collision of many precise tasks. (Antin *Conversation* 46)

The underlying comment may be self-reflexive and providing tools to understand his own practice of improvisation in the talk-poem. In "Some Questions about Modernism," Antin mentions John Cage, and Jackson Mac Low who carry out similar experiments in procedural participative production (37); in his introduction to the volume dedicated to Allan Kaprow's work, Antin reminisces about joint events in which he and Mac Low took part[8]; well before that, he had paid close attention to Jackson Mac Low's *The Pronouns* when interviewed by Barry Alpert for the *Vort* issue of 1975:

'The Pronouns' was a kind of flickering machine that kept moving around and around building provisional intelligent meanings that would rapidly crumble and that Jackson would construct and reconstruct out of this rubble of obligatory words he could modify only by changing their grammatical relations--turning a verb to a noun or a noun to an adjective and inserting the pronoun in the place he happened to feel like--as the receiver of action or the dealer, so to speak. (*Vort* 15)

Similarly to the remarks on Kaprow, the comment on Mac Low and the "intelligence" of decomposing/recomposing constructions is not solely an approach to the disconcerting methods of Mac Low's works: it indirectly provides more clues to understand Antin's own practice, at a turning point marked by the advent of the talk-poem as an increasingly scripted procedure.

David Huntsperger has thus pointed out the political and cultural implications of proceduralism in the earlier poetry of Antin, notably in his close reading of "Novel Poem," a text composed through the systematic reading-through of pulp fiction or "trashy novels" (Antin's words) and appropriation of citations. The process

---

[8] "The first time I saw Allan in action was at a performance of Karlheinz Stockhausen's opera *Originale* in Carnegie Recital Hall, for which Karlheinz had persuaded Allan to play and act as the director. I don't know what the German version is like, but in the American version that Allan seems to have put together himself with a little help from Charlotte Moorman, it was a carnivalesque affair with lots of things going on at the same time, lots of props–ladders and scaffoldings, a trapeze hanging from the ceiling and lots of colorful people–the "originals" of the title–wandering in and out. There was a kind of audience, mostly on the stage at the end of the hall, while the action was on the floor. Jackson Mac Low and I, who were recruited to simply read poetry no matter what happened, were seated at the edge of the stage." (Antin *in* Kelley xii)

follows previous attempts, in *the november exercises* with snippets from the news, or in part III of the "Black Plague" which Antin describes as "an arrangement of words taken from a translation of Wittgenstein's *Philosophical Investigations*" (Antin *definitions* 38). Huntsperger focuses on the way procedures of poetic composition thematize and critique "the larger conditions of production within an era of American hegemony," making "intellectual labor— either implicitly or explicitly—the primary concern of the literary work" (Huntsperger 3): this leads him to read Antin's intention as underscoring "the creativity required by the act of reading itself, which is always both an act of consumption and production of meaning" (Huntsperger 83).

Following up on what Huntsperger sees as Antin "further expanding the possibilities of proceduralism itself" in the openly procedural experiments of the 1960s and early 1970s (76), one can see that the talk-poem prolongs and seals this commitment to proceduralism. It does this in a paradoxical way, since the work primarily seems to fall into the category of live performance and improvisation. Yet from having helped David organize several of his talks I know that there were fixed conditions to be fulfilled for the performance to take place: the unscripted part was carefully framed by an addition of factors (the definition of place and occasion well ahead of the event; an evaluation of the expected audience; room organization and the visible presence of the recorder; no chair...). Through the production of this type of constraints, Antin's work evolves in a manner akin to the procedural inventiveness of Jackson Mac Low, Allan Kaprow, or Jerome Rothenberg, all of them friends and collaborators.

This is also what might account for the closeness between Antin and French Oulipo poet Jacques Roubaud, which Marjorie Perloff underlines in her text "In Memoriam: David Antin (1932-2016)," calling them "kindred spirit[s]" (179). Roubaud finds interest in Antin's talk-poem because it is procedural. This proceduralism does not contradict the idea of Antin as "an American pragmatist" (Perloff 179) as it helps in fact define this pragmatism. Antin brings about a fundamental recognition of the empirical nature of poetic form. The claim had been made before the talk-poem for flexible poetic forms as a pragmatic response to changeable conditions, and Antin's talk-poem responds to that claim while countering the criticism against "free" form: flexibility does not imply to renounce form altogether. The talk-poems are simultaneously unique in their form and iterative in their successive instances because they are the results of a single procedure that is in part scripted and in part conditioned by exterior factors: they emerge as the form of flexible form.

The device of the talk-poem aims at accounting for the irreducible contingency of existence and of creation: it hinges on a procedure whereby the conditions of composition have been identified and assessed. Some of these conditions have been procedurally determined and scripted: an anticipated time and location, the recorder, the presence of an audience, the process of transcription, and formatting in print. Meanwhile, other variables are ostensibly put into play: the inscription of the moment in individual and collective history, the specificity of a place, the interaction with the audience, the demands of expository coherence in writing, the unspecified yet enforced constraint of about an hour's performing/reading time for each talk-poem.

As one can infer from these enumerations that make up the main characteristics of the talk-poem, the overarching main rule or constraint, to take up Oulipian terminology, the common denominator to all the items in the series is time. This is the intuition of Jennifer Scappettone in the conclusion to her comparison between Antin and Rothenberg. She maps out the convergence and divergence of two works with apparently very different options:

> The poetic act emerges as a pulse of potentially infinite rapprochement and estrangement— until time, for the moment, runs out. (Scappettone 785)

The metaphor of "a pulse" used by Scappettone is significant, as it crystallizes the iterative dimension of the compositional modes, their regularity, their implied perceptiveness to the context as well as their essential vital urgency.

The ethics of conceptualism

Recent assessments of the work have thus shown the convergence between Antin's work and the work of younger artists. This is the case with some photographers and videasts from the 2016 exhibition at the San Diego Museum of Contemporary Art. The catalogue to the exhibition features Antin's 1976 "remembering recording representing," from which I quoted initially. This talk is a landmark in Antin's work, as it thematizes the parallel workings of memory and of the talk-poem. In the 2016 San Diego exhibition, Antin is included among artists "diverse in their approaches, [that] shared an orientation toward conceptualism and a desire to challenge modern orthodoxies" (Dawsey "Introduction" 18). This "conceptualism" dating back to the 1970s takes us up to the present, and present instances of "conceptual writing." The definition may shift as the term moves into the foreseeable future of poetic work, but it may also offer tools for a rephrasing of poetic practices in less negative (non-modern) or relative (post-modern), thus more proactive/productive terms.

As William Spurlock had already noticed in his introductory notes to the 1979 Santa Barbara Museum of Art exhibit entitled *Dialogue/Discourse/Research,* a key issue in Antin's processes is the achievement of a specific state of "readiness." Readiness implies much more anticipation and intentionality than the fantasies of spontaneous explosions of fascinating intelligence and wit may allow for.

> Antin's process is to prepare himself with knowledge about his subject by spending several days "on location," researching and dialoguing with it as a resource for his performance. When he enters the gallery for the *Dialogue*, his artistic process is complete to the point of formalization. His resources include what he has learned from the location and the linguistic concerns at the base of all his work. With all in readiness, the dialogue is structured and the experience manifested at the moment of presentation. In this sense, the *Dialogue* is in the recent tradition of site-specific art. His work is conditioned by the circumstances of his immediate environment. (Spurlock in *Dialogue* 4)

Thus, a twofold dialectics is at work in the production of the talk-poem, that rests on this achievement of "readiness." It involves preparation and scripting well beyond the mere awareness of a day and place for a planned event in the calendar: the "site-specificity" of Spurlock's comment implies a siting of the poem in an intellectual and mental place, that may be as systematic, and much less random than expected. This mental and intellectual siting of the poem impacts the text as strongly and significantly as the practical and material conditions of its production, and is part of the procedure.

A way to this mental space is through David Antin's notebooks: they abound in exploratory lists that move from conventional phrases to uncanny expressions (figure 1), that create connections between words through substitution and permutation (figure 2, but also a feature of figure 1), that keep testing linguistic organizations and foreground potential connections that will generate "infinite" possibilities "until time [...] runs out" (Scappettone 785). When the notations span three pages and two different notebooks (figures 3 and 4), they encourage the reader to deconstruct the boundaries of single volumes.

After having destabilized the line, the stanza, and the page through the form of the talk-poem, Antin performs this paring-down to the "radical coherency" of poetic work as he intends it: in a poetics of relation and sociability ("friend"), through repetition ("accumulate"), attention ("recognize"), conservation ("save"), maybe some form of salvation ("save"), to ensure transmission for an elusive distant voice ("telephone"). Indeed, the process of defamiliarization that distances us from linguistic configurations pervades all levels of the work from the "atomic" level of lettrist games (figure 2) to the "cosmic" level of the book as "gravitational center":

> So I seem to remember writing the name of each of my pieces
> on a small slip of paper and putting them in a pile from which
> I extracted one at a time and considered it for inclusion or
> exclusion. Once I had my eight inclusions I had to figure out the
> placement, which was easy for the first one and the last two in
> the book. The first serves as an imaginary origin piece and the
> last two gave my image of a "personal" piece. Then there was
> "the sociology of art" [...] And so it went with this notion of the
> book as a kind of solar system with a gravitational center and a
> set of planetary talks orbiting around it. (Antin *Selected* 379)

The lists for a contents table in figure 5 illustrate this method of composition as it affects the composition of the book, inclusions and exclusions, and the attention paid to the re-contextualization of the poem in the "site-specific" conditions of a printed volume.

It also incites us to look back at the organizations of Antin's poetics as deliberately transitional, calculated yet changeable formations. The texts conceptualize this condition of contingency, provisionality and contiguity; art's configurations are alternative linguistic systems that "take a crack at" organization (Antin "remembering recording representing" *in* Dawsey 190). Disconcertingly however, they constantly threaten to return to the random units and sequences of "pieces on [a] small slip[s] of paper [...] in a pile" (Antin *Selected* 379). But listings such as those exhibited in the archive but also in a wide number of published poems show us the poet listening to the "real," along with us, rather than voicing it for us to listen and hear.

"whos list(en)ing out there"

So as we expand the "domain" (Antin "Some Questions" 37) of the work, to include all of the texts beyond the apparent heterogeneity of the media they use (from tape to printed volume), we might not "hear anything [we]'re not hearing now," to recall Marjorie Perloff's anecdote (Perloff 179): yet Antin's apparently dismissive statement to the impatient listener is programmatic in its assertion of charted yet non-prescriptive poetic modes of production/reception. If all forego limiting expectations in favor of preparation and readiness, there may be hope for a more adequate response to David Antin's poetic and ethical commitment, a generalization of his own example-based definition of "the basic form of irony": "a kind of destabilization" that "doesn't stop you but [it] destabilizes meaning." (Antin *in* McHale 111). Antin's language games and art engage in destabilizing modes of listing and listening. The open-ended cumulative processes of composition, the refusal to commit to the singularity of a medium, or the unicity of a one-sided truth participate in a process of desacralization of artistic media, and of experimentation in a poetics of conversation and communication:

> For example, we are making use of computer software to converse in a manner that I somewhat described as a combination of the eighteenth century and the twentieth. You propose that its possibilities seem very different from the face-to-face communication of the oral tradition. And you're right. But so is snail mail, and the notebook in which we compose our own thoughts, and the tiny audiotape recorder and even smaller digital recorders that have replaced them. The visual effect of true face-to-face communication is I think less important than the belief that someone out there is really listening. (Antin *Selected* 381).

This implies to conceive of the talk-poem as a combined process of composition whereby the "someone out there [is] really listening" is not just a passive member of the audience. That "someone" is a dynamic agent that subsumes all these instances that we categorize rashly from poets, to readers, or even critics, and constitutes them into non-dogmatic, provisional yet effective communication-based communities. Under these conditions, then, and as we reconsider David Antin's multiple list(en)ings, we can recognize the painful irony of his statement that there is "nothing else coming" (Antin evoked by Perloff 179). Often letting people know that they can leave, and stop listening, David Antin conversely voices hope that the listening will persist as we list our "second thoughts" (Antin "remembering recording representing" *in* Dawsey 190).

Works Cited:

All quotations and reproductions from published and unpublished work of David Antin by kind permission of Eleanor Antin Copyright 2017.

Alpert, Barry. "Post-Modern Oral Poetry: Buckminster Fuller, John Cage, and David Antin." *Boundary 2* III 3 (1975) 665-682.

Antin, David and Charles Bernstein. *A Conversation with David Antin.* New York: Granary Books, 2002.

Antin, David. "Is There a Postmodernism?" *Bucknell Review* XXV 2 (1980) 127-135.

Antin, David. "Modernism and Postmodernism: Approaching the Present in American Poetry." *Boundary 2* (1972) 98-133.

Antin, David. "radical coherency." *O.ARs (Coherence)* I (1981) 177-191.

Antin, David. "Some Questions About Modernism." *Occident* VIII (1974) 7-38.

Antin, David. "The Stranger at the Door," *in* Marjorie Perloff, ed. *Postmodern Genres.* Norman: University of Oklahoma Press, 1989. 229-247.

Antin, David. *Code of Flag Behaviour.* Los Angeles: Black Sparrow, 1968.

Antin, David. *Definitions.* New York: Caterpillar, 1967.

Antin, David. *How Long is the Present: Selected Talk Poems of David Antin.* Stephen Fredman, ed. Albuquerque: University of New Mexico Press, 2014.

Antin, David. *whos listening out there.* College Park: Sun & Moon Press, 1979.

Dawsey, Jill, ed. *The Uses of Photography: Art, Politics, and the Re-invention of a Medium.* La Jolla, CA: Museum of Contemporary Art San Diego, 2016.

Deleuze, Gilles. *Kafka: pour une littérature mineure*. Paris: Éditions de Minuit, 1975.

Derrida, Jacques. *Of Grammatology*. Baltimore: Johns Hopkins University Press, 1976.

Goldsmith, Kenneth. *Day*. Great Barrington (MA): The Figures, 2003.

Hornick, Lita. *David Antin/Debunker of the "Real."* Putnam Valley, NY: Swollen Magpie Press, 1979.

Huntsperger, David W. *Procedural Form in Postmodern American Poetry: Berrigan, Antin, Silliman, and Hejinian*. New York: Palgrave Macmillan, 2010.

Kelley, Jeff. *Childsplay: The Art of Allan Kaprow*. Berkeley: University of California Press, 2004.

Lyotard, Jean-François. *La Condition postmoderne (1979). The Postmodern Condition*. Trans. James Bennington and Brian Massumi. Minneapolis: University of Minnesota Press, 1984.

McHale, Brian, ed. "Talking Narrative: A Conversation with David Antin." *Narrative* XII 1 (2004) 93-115.

Paul, Sherman. *So To Speak, Rereading David Antin*. London: Binnacle Press, 1982.

Perloff, Marjorie. "In Memoriam: David Antin (1932-2016)." *Critical Inquiry* 44 (2017) 175-179.

Scappettone, Jennifer. "Tuning as Lyricism: The Performances of Orality in the Poetics of Jerome Rothenberg and David Antin." *Critical Inquiry* 37 (2011) 782-786.

Selected Recordings from the Getty Digital Collections. http://rosettaapp.getty.edu:1801/delivery/ DeliveryManagerServlet?dps_pid=IE520067 (accessed 27 Oct. 2017)

Spurlock, William. "Notes on the Exhibition" in *Dialogue/Discourse/ Research (David Antin, Eleanor Antin, Helen Mayer Harrison/ Newton Harrison, Fred Lonidier, Barbara Strasen)*. Catalogue. Santa Barbara Museum of Art (Sept. 1-Oct. 28, 1979) 4-18.

The David Antin Papers. The Getty Research Institute, Los Angeles.

Vort 7 (David Antin and Jerome Rothenberg). Barry Alpert, ed. (1975).

Watten, Barrett. *Questions of Poetics: Language Writing and its Consequences*. Iowa City: University of Iowa Press, 2016.

Williams, William Carlos. *The Embodiment of Knowledge*. New York : New Directions, 1974.

Figure 1 (*Antin Papers* Series 1 Box 11 Folder 4):

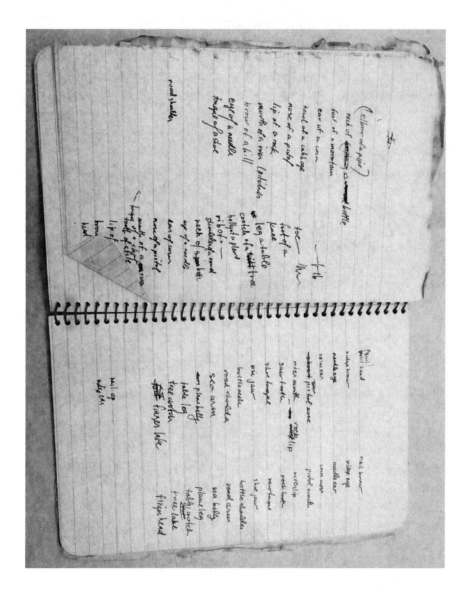

Figure 2 (*Antin Papers* Series 1 Box 9 Folder 4):

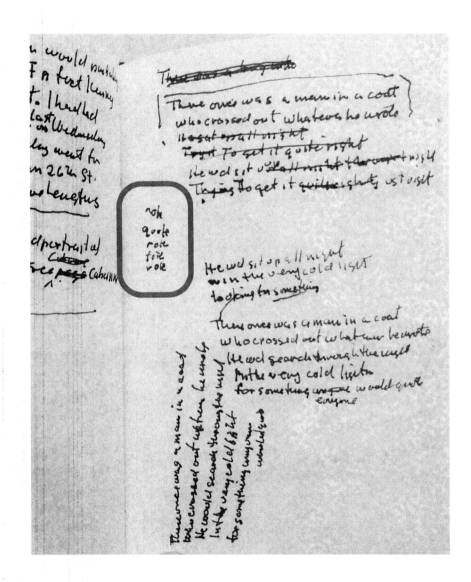

Figures 3, 4 (*Antin Papers* Series 1 Box 11 Folder 4):

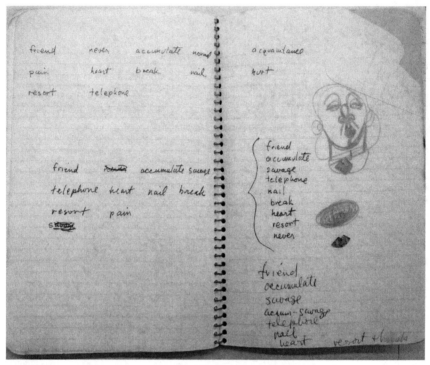

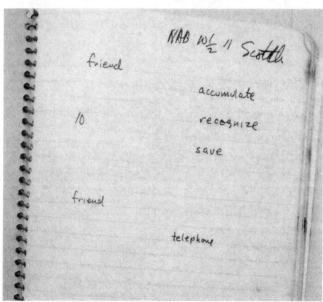

Figure 5 (*Antin Papers* Series 1 Box 11 Folder 9)

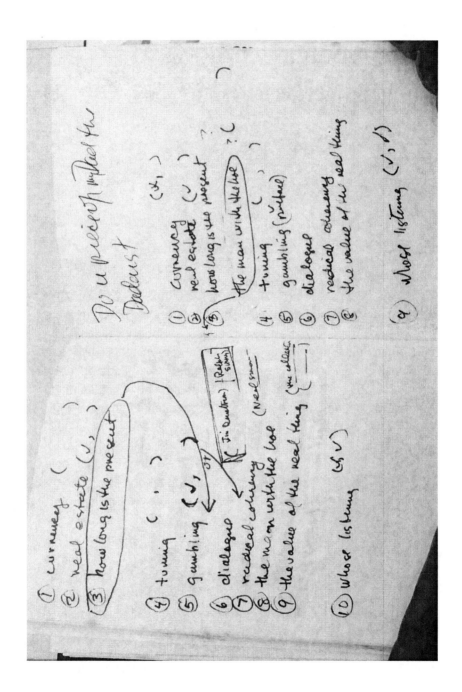

David Antin and Robert Duncan in San Diego

Stephen Fredman

In 1972 (July 10?) I observed a colloquy between two poetic thinkers who were to profoundly affect my own poetics: Robert Duncan and David Antin. In the early 1970s, when I first met Antin, his talk poems were making a big splash. He was the first person to stage a "poetry reading" as an occasion to stand up in front of an audience and think out loud, without any written notes. He would often begin by talking about the details of preparing his tape recorder to capture what he said, and then he would continue remarking on events leading up to his being in that particular room, and slowly it would dawn on people that *this* was the poem. He was a bit of a stand-up comedian, a bit of a peripatetic philosopher, and a bit of a wise-guy storyteller from Brooklyn. After the event, Antin would transcribe his talking neither as verse nor prose but rather as units of utterance separated by spaces and with no justified margins. Duncan, whom I'd met back in 1967, saw these informal talk poems as a disturbing challenge to what poetry could be. In the solar system of California poetry in the early 1970s, Duncan and Antin were large planets, although they seemed to orbit each other more like matter and anti-matter.

Oddly, one of the things that united them was that each claimed a heritage from Romanticism, their definitions of which diverged radically. For Duncan, Romanticism inaugurated the primacy of imagination in poetic thinking. And for him, imagination is the faculty of apprehending cosmic or natural forms that organically underlie poetic intuition and poetic forms. For Antin, Romanticism marked a new historical epoch, in which human beings invent their own phenomenological reality, a reality that in turn makes existential demands upon us. He saw the forms of poetry as trivial distractions when compared to the unpredictability and challenge of being addressed directly by someone talking and of trying to figure out something hitherto not understood.

When Duncan came to read at UCSD, it was a moment for each man to decide if his sense of poetry might include the other. Each had a comprehensive conception of poetry as a way of thinking, a capacious mode that could include many types of knowledge but seemingly only one overriding perspective (his own).

After the reading we repaired to the house the Antins were renting on the bluffs overlooking the ocean in Solana Beach. David's wife, Eleanor, a multimedia artist obsessed with narrative went off to the bedroom to watch soap operas, leaving me, the tremulous young man, alone with two imposing figures.

In the longish, somewhat narrow living room, Duncan and Antin seated themselves opposite one another, with myself in the middle—like a line judge in a professional ping pong match, in which the players stand many feet back from respective ends of the table and let fly fearsome volleys. They were, in fact, two of the most loquacious, unpredictable, and uninterruptible talkers I have ever heard, and I felt my head whip back and forth as though watching them lob grenades across the net.

It was hard to believe my fortune as the lone, awestruck spectator to this unrivaled verbal display. Once and for all I saw that not only is poetry for real but it's played for keeps.

Over years of discussions with these poets, I learned that poetics is a mode of thinking that can include *everything.* For Duncan, this conviction was based in part on a faith inherited from Freud that everything is meaningful—even slips, mistakes, the childish, the everyday, dreams, the occult, the perverted—anything human beings are capable of thinking and doing must be brought on board and measured within a poetics. In Antin's belief the poet is the person capable of confronting whatever happens and thinking with it as it does, someone not driven to resolve an occasion into already accepted categories but who lets it interact promiscuously with other facts, attitudes, circumstances—thus making them all surprising. Duncan was a vast metaphor machine, setting everything in relation to everything else along what he called "an absolute scale of resemblance and disresemblance." Antin was intent on extending the cultural project inaugurated by Russian Futurism and Marcel Duchamp and renewed by John Cage, Allan Kaprow, and the Fluxus artists—that of making the ordinary and the everyday strange through, in his case, an interrogation of language.

The largest lesson I took from this encounter is that poetic thinking is challenging because it's holistic (big) or transgressive (unexpected). It doesn't respect normal boundaries, such as those between media, between intellectual realms, between body, mind, and spirit. Get ready for unforeseen leaps. Learn to take them in stride.

Two excerpts from
For the Ride

Alice Notley

(For the Ride is a long narrative poem in which, after a global disaster, a group of people board an ark called Radio Free Ark, and voyage into another level of being. Their speech collapses somewhat, and they stop using conventional pronouns, opting largely for the pronoun "one." The narrator's consciousness is "One." In these excerpts, they enter a deserted city where mysterious word-ridden things happen to them. There is as a given an "anthology" whose poems are interspersed amid the story; and there are illustrations made of words.)

VI *Disembarkment*

One's found the lost city no one was ever in
made of words One's selecting, city extends from the Ark, as it goes
  along road of the dead, ragged
unforeseen being one is
                always past or is, angelic idyllic
                find it in some words, there is nothing else left
                everything ended, one watches fall
                human systems, not more humans but words

                escaping with One into Chaos, mixage
                And One gets mixed right into the cauldron
                or is it more like a chameleon
                rumpled and least

nothing is most, here come words
those One loved or used with a wrist no wrist here, how come words are?
  because One is How Because mind's what there is over all in out
  prove it. what one knows, all science, is from In
            from knowing with a mind, who else's
                        One's the ancient of Detail
            it all One is under and up

  Ark beneath the hemlock sky glides full and cogent
(in a sense -- the sense of *this*) O City
    abandoned where no One has been
  to take the call and Foundation. One
    covered in combs, comb out the words now
  Come into *this* doubtful Grace.

Then, where are the ones of the ark? Ark is landing in faux port;
faux's the ark, faux's any thing but One -- how come One's not so faux?
One's the light within, all one knows. Only dependable chose,
that there's this steadyflamelike self; entering the faux city,
with One's amoeboid entourage, projections babbling, afraid . . .
don't know how to act, no standards since everything collapsèd . . .

Do the ones have words for new act? énième fois cosmical start?
Pouring out of One, way they do -- march down l'Allée des Morts now,

are the ones really deceased? asks Wideset eyes. In sense, Qui
replies, previous world is gone. What is this ghost burg? -- Shaker.
It's the city after it's dead futurely, ready for ones --
Whah? Gives one creeps, say soul suckers. Everyone's already dead,

One says, all ones are au courant. Why only one tense needed. --
Why be born then? -- Nobody knows. -- Maybe One can find out this time.

Really don't get it! -- Shaker. It's some city, in future from now,
dead. -- Why? -- Because, it, is, futurely. Ones 'll be dead so it's dead.

One, says one, is covered with sudden words. One's composed of the new
or at least layered with. One can't read them. Can see some but they crawl.
One is now different. What language is One in? One speaks English --

or is it a new form, another langue, English ever shifting --
one's hands, knees, or are they those, are they blurred words, unstable
          lovelies?

Need to read each other? Parts one calls up, from beside One's own ears.
One can probably help. Tree still at work. One consists of word tree,
in a sense -- each one is that poem, shifting, breeze-mutated,
blown into new shapes by one soul current among the ones. Not to
be confusèd with consciousness, one's own. One's own soul, that is.

Parts one works for the One. Still. Suggesting replacements and fixtures
messaged telepathically from grapevine -- hah! -- tree. This city's covered one
more quickly than one can keep up with. Bypassed. Have to learn what's up.
It's happening faster than the old system. The words are swarming now.

Covered by the body of words -- a body of gliding new words: Who?
One is the same One . . . No, one isn't. Don't know what One's gonna say.

Je suis coupable. Erregina. One refuses all the pasts . . .
One is guilty of razing nature. Which -- nature -- isn't gendered . . .
only one's eyes were -- Have no real eyes. Seen has its own declension,
chart: you seen -- object. Seer -- nomen. Delimnèd . . .
delineated, it doesn't know that it's defined being seen --
how fair can that be? One sees you-seen. One sees one-seen? Abolished:

the wires -- one's not wired, hard or hardly. See one, all one sees are words.
Palabras of fate, if one's fated -- nam fatalis: no country
in new ordinem: France is dead now. How one loved thee! Love remains?
Energetically, molecular? No, parts of scattered verbiage.

One's caused to stand here, by what if One's consciousness is free, thirsty,
is One? One-seen, e.g. Wideset -- with thine own consciousness, too, libre.

One uses I when suddenly one's I, the inmost soul of one.
I, Wideset? . . . not that. The blue sea's green somewhere in past and I clean.
Ent'ring the city imagined by ones to come now? the next ville?
That's too fixed for one; so the words keep shifting that would define one --

they can't! But ones agree to choose the words to bring into new world:
do they instantly take over this one? I, soul of me, Wideset . . .

to you the layer superficial, of my sensed response to world,
my reasoning, my naming of fact as if it were -- implore that
you remain in flux, for forever, that none define one!

In winter time more bruised dogs down who and him again, duck nostalgia.
Talk like that's better. Drawer upon rubber, tell would she couldn't.
Would one couldn't? Oh, couldn't meanwhile atmosphere ends, unique.
Is unique a thing? Verb quits as known. Need it not to define
the past, because no one is in it. It's conjectural like now

as ones procede along in present no need to catch it so bad.

Don't get what's happening, Shaker whispers to his hand, with word HAND on it,
also THE ROSE HOSED ABIDING I WILL OW. Think one's the tree!

Qui says, Yes but one's more than lucky -- incontrovertibly one.

Are ones choosing these words after all, or are they choosing the ones?
One feels as if one's being chosen. Tickets, please. Mine 're fingers:
If I have fingers, do I have to say I, mine? These hand . . .
"The rose hosed abiding I will ow" is the poem of my hand:
MY hand, not another's. One begins to understand the problem . . .
Shaker finishes. One's dumbstruck. One could be anything at all.

Maybe ones don't understand this city, says the One, not yet.
It's gone, already . . . but ones are it . . . Are it becomingly, now?

Soul suckers: how can ones take it over if the terms keep changing?
Exactly, says One. Anyone's a new poem today. All's well.

Time as the Stretching Out of a Lantern Cutout

       minepeace
       denied
       . by you .

map made by who   declare
    end of world . . . . that's poem
    bottoms out . . . . there
    : ya fated oo la . . . . says who
    now turns out one dreams it . nothing ever here
    . why not any map of any place

       walk to here -- what's walk
          . . don't get it
            . get our own
           no   'us'

       then what ones here
       said to me
       some many
       people
       essence

(don't let any one take over. Even if it's a 'part' of one? That's right)
Deal no ego. System unstable.

       (From the Anthology)

THIS WHEN PRESSED EMITS SOUND

does one know Chance
it's each
perhaps. Necessitas?
as
    . . dragon

      . imagined

         . like these words?

      stay bodiless

      don't call

      One thing

   . sick for a beauty one remembers
   seacoast real
   ever the Ark
          remains with ones, transparent foundation

      . .   tree . glyph
      does   'nt . matter
      memory's fluid
   paint . . ed . bird . dawn . same
born uncreature   palladian
      .   .   . from foreheads
      Eyelids closed, see inside .

                              (From the Anthology)

VII *Becoming Poems*

Does One act or is One handled by past ones unthinkingly then --
What's placing words on One? Can't One read them? What poem is One now?
Eyes but whose float rounded in a brown space: teeth in the space and nose
because One knows of the nose -- hair-feathers green -- oh why not look like
        that?
A second face in one's heart place. How does One see this self come towards

with hands of painted nails, maroon, holding -- why hold something like that?
        -- cloths

covered with gibberish, how does One know? Because this proposèd
personage One could seem, floating parts like the almost familiar
loosely strung, comes from within One as does everything concentrated

in massed piece: can One reject it? It'll be sad, mad; how tedious, this!

Tell One who thou art, one! -- One ist thou, One -- So what, One's an any . . .

Welcome me! -- Why bother? One wants to be word, not a puppet creatured
with strung pieces anciens . . . Dissolve to True, One wants to light up,
new, but necessarily, what One is. Then falls apart, those parts,

and more words illisible swarm on space where One supposes One is --
territory of moi's stretching outwards from what painted, candled
reflection -- oh not that -- origination, in itself the source?
Dost thou get it, reflet, undermined? Grâce aux renseignements, I,

One, keep babbling to ones, waiting till One can read what's going on . . .

My entourage be near, shadowed and tense. Stay loyal to those,
from the times together, but One's ruthless -- quality essential.
I'll read these words or else. Art inventing them; are ones making them?
Wideset asks? -- How could One? They're from pooled minds, as is figure
        collapsed

of Oneself that endures . . . from the future? Qui, canst thou speak for One,
who the fuck ever thou art of Oneself? No, *you* have to do it.

Read the damned words on the body of bliss. *You* have to read all those.
Stop asking questions and peruse the verbiage though it's not too new.
Why can't One face this sweet language of stars, points of light
                indépendants?

One -- on trouve sa place? no not that. One's the origin of now.
Thou dost not know the beginning, e'en of the words thou art,
Ark, or poem, One, first maker. What exactly does one mean?

To be in active dominion, to be in charge of the hosts
on One's skin -- no skin -- to be first, each moment to be the one,
each of the ark's words: escaped, ear, despair phoned of blue wrists
for a compulsion of dawn, medicine, frown, or rapax.
Look it up. Qualities cease within one but not their letters.
One's a shifter's recognition, is that it? asks the Shaker.

BEHOLD SOME BODIES SHIFTING

.
this think
dawn without sun
. grey One's eyes of
. the shifters. One of
. never of   .   see One's form
. One's moving word thighs
. feet tis . . .
. the cut-out pacers
not cauterized
my worth lone oriel
. inspired
aye One is epic
. sane One moves word limbs
across grey city now
discontinued
giving slowly back line of eros
bitter   .   trick   .   okay
. . from within One
. don't One want
.   that . mad
. others chose too
. have to let ones
as One walks now
to long street
oh so twi
lit god One

leg of
astra; narrator,
groupwisely, the
ones
chose some
Words on One

```
            The poet is
            the original
            birds cry to.
            There are no
                birds
                left . . .
        Can the ones call each other
      poet as
      pronoun? 'Poet are fair, are real'
      poet says                    The ones 're
       to poet,         ial what-      reflected
       'poet love       ever it can    upon by
       poet.' Or, po-   be called.     no light but
       et are a jerk,   Time's un-     of words in
       poet am bad.     glued, it      this grey
        this is a       isn't that     city.  Poets
           f  o  s      that One (Poet)  by
        h  o  r  a      glitters within   n   s  n  o  t
        a  r  m  k      en morçeaux       e   i  e  r   h
        n     '  e      ou cum spiri-     c   t  '  m   e
        d  f  s         tu auditionis --  e   y.  s
                        hearing but       s       i   e
                        what vibrates?      o  f  n   s s e n t-
                        Not air as the
                        ones have ever
                        defined it, or
                        space -- What
                        are poets, Why
                        are ones alive?
           foot-            of the
           loose            dead?
         in the street   Help Ones, Ether
```

One's not different from source of the words cast upon one like light.

Change the sub: isn't there some sort of *light* here anyway? asks One --
But so grey! Wideset says. Can't tell if it's light, or some other vibrant;
changing one's appearances, seen and maybe the heard --
Or is that what one does, sees and listens, speaks, within this dreamy world?

One finds frescoes about, as in the glyph, Look! they're creaturely -- there --
terrifyingly deserted like ones. Are ones deserted? asks kid,
dead France's -- In a sense. Are ones deserted of oneselves? asks kid.
Ones make ones, then leave ones. All in the past. Ones deserted of selves . . .

Shaker says, Don't get it. One, even you, a deserted artwork,
deserted building or walls of a once-made, Wideset says to one.

But, it's more like the ones are the very selves. Maybe the selves are left,
left like frescoes then found. As if in time? What is the time of this?
What source word light or thought? Soul suckers tense. Ones must be ones'
          own gods

forgotten as the gods. Thus deserted. Beauty of the face like on the walls:

every thing's a muted, worn color coming to life again. Look!
The colors suddenly burn into non-eyes of the ones who are words . . .

for only word-covered ones see the future and the past of ones.

Are ones better for this, this arrival? Tired of asking questions,

mutters the Parts one: point of being in coma if one's uncertain.
Let ones choose certain. Soul suckers tense still: Ones can't judge anything.
Nothing is familiar. Did ones bring "judge"? asks Wideset. Probably . . .

Still haven't invented a new language. Maybe ones are speaking
it, Ones says, not knowing. Qui adds, *In the mouth:* If one's here it's new.
Ones stare at each other, masses of words, in the old future dream.

The ghosts are all in the words (one is there) or as on the plaster wall.
     exuded   in the

from   in the

Memories of thee, materialism, when the ones loving
    dost   I
    thou   mem, one
    mem   mems   how many *things*   for sale

items, remember *things*? The soul suckers recall careers, sal'ries --
prizes like cold grass grow on hackneyed thoughts, chef d'oeuvres aren't
here: the commando's One: One tolerates this triste confusion
her   comptable   one one   tall
bleeds   bleeds   from wha   no
down   rightness , why one   height

where it lies visible to one's grey eyes. Or brown, as birds. Extinct
on all walls sing the sky. When is that, of life soul-suck, where's on top?
Ones want to be *on top*, soul suckers cry. Where is the medium?

    whe   is   medium,
    within   motional   eyes
    in   med   new wild-

erness, enchanted, One, and One says, One's found One's element. Mome,
moment. Not quite fixèd. One's hair, one's eyes, one's hearing immater-
ial. One is the source of. For One comes back. Was I once a bird?

Nothing varies but the light: One means something else but what is it?
that One's in and is of, émitteur quand même. Or the sound of it.
chruso chrusotera. Thrust out a word, just to keep talking, One.
aptete pur. Doesn't -- oesn't -- matter. Claw at paint for Xaos'
sake. Nothing varies but light, or the gradation of the thinking --
    seems
  sk love .
    di
  one is tossed
One seeks confirmation nonetheless, says One, of the reality
of One's langue, tongue of chaos. Can ones speak it? All ones now have left.
Qui begins to growl; is it words? Why not? the voyagers say.
Then the breasted soul sucker demands, One must see, must see more.

Of a sudden Qui who's growling's emergent from fresco --

Does one look like something now, ma'am? One sees One's interior,
zounds! or sounds, One's shamanic force, mystery's on the near wall:
Qui is in right there in the wall, right with those painted animals:

Is One's interior a winged jaguar or snake abstracted,
yes perhaps anything fierce goes -- fierce in the utmost chaos,
isn't any quality part, One beist moi, a mélange
and a purity. What thou sayst, from Qui or who is red, blue,
yellow and white, *is* eyes if ones make out these marbles dedans,

in the assemblage of my forms -- I'm the, your, my: bloody mouth,
reddest mouth in the universe. Let's remake some of Being.
Only have words existing, sweethearts that's enough to go.
And if one tries to suck one's soul, will seal you in a black wall.

Parts of new universe are one's words. What some one says is the case.

Do ones have bodies? asks Wideset. Well, says Wall Qui, one sees one there,
covered with words, but with those eyes. Why? What does one do with them
in this greyness? One's some fed up. Everything's based on before . . .
There was never an origin: creation, evolution,
All is poppycock! In the mids, interlocking is our truth . . .

Like, ones like two eyes hanging there. *Like*? Yeah ones like it, Qui says --
Isn't shamanic, to *like* it. Oh right, live up to the word . . .

op boppy dabra, beat a drum, dumbdumbs in lightless neutral,
goose grey lack of happenstantial space, place or after math of.
Rendering of planet useless to the species ones were callèd.

Now to call it Loquacious Souls. Dead species covered with words.
One -- yes -- brings ones back from the death, *to* this here moment thrilling,
charged with what? Not believing things. With skeptical randomness.

Ones now proceed randomly as pleases. One don't want to think more.

Let's call this grey stuff light, says the One. The Celestial Presence.

Sudden shafts appear gold everywhere, play props, a little rigid,
aren't they? comments Qui. Where are they from? (Who cares who asks?)
      Nowhere,

like where one is in fact -- oh no fact here -- making a bunch of facts.

Are ones still in the glyph? Where else but there. Of a sudden thick piles,
cuttings, are at one's feet. More fuckin words, says the Shaker, like me.
Bits, more of pastness. How one's concrete, by pulling it along . . .
ghan builu . . . enter war. Oh brother that wasn't too brilliant, huh
ronmentalists are already argu. Papers flutter, a wind
there's a wind in nowhere. *dent to minister man; with foreign lead;*
financial; dominates; degradation of fores. Don't want these ones . . .
Already had the fuckers didn't one. *Main index down by 7*

Let's accept numbers. Then Wideset cries, Oh one's lost difference
between one and others. Can't perceive it, though there's a voice from
      mouth --
Whose? It's one's? Is one located at all? One's mass is slippery --

One sees your wideset eyes, two balls floating in pile of stuff . . .
What does one need to be? Pull self together around digestive
tubes, oh that's just more words. If one eats it's off to side. I'm not it.

Don't have to. Don't be *that.* What to become? Wideset is muttering.
One's my mom, says her kid. Yeah but what else? Are the ones too dead for
relationships du corps? It's that one don't perceive the body parts the same
      way.
One came out of the one? When? One doesn't have that past anymore . . .
Hysteric. It isn't happening, now. Thou art thyself, one thinks . . .

Am I? I am my one . . . Pull thyself together, literally --

Does one want a body? Volition has nothing to do with that.
One could want to kill it, etcetera. Are ones going to kill?
Have taken selves to place of decision. One *sees* oneself as what,

as not stuck together. Hold pose a sec, says who me, the no pose.
Far as one can take it. Has one lost it? Is that good, after all?

Can't get rid of reasoner -- observer. *I don't want to be you.*
Or is it that one's not. Sick of questions. Pull pieces of one back
more less together. Don't care what one looks like, am not eye-owned.

Big as mind, body parts merge into void -- cosmic contained in mind --
ego sense dissipates, words for these states glitter and swarm on one,

never still. Never *still*! They are the bits, cells of thine existence,

have to be changeable, somewhat stable; one changes in chaos,
that manages itself, that is the one. I am of it -- one is --

Wideset's eyes glowering, more apart now. Can still see all of ones!
Ability to see simply exists -- Has always been somewhere.
No way to evolve without preexistence, assholes! Pre-seeing,
post-seeing. Existence of thing posits thing. A kind of logic.

The Automobile
our Narrative

David Bromige

How slowly the highway delivers the new
at sixty, the mountains always slipping
away from us, and our perceptions tiring
of telling us we are puny, reeling from
fixing on a few fence-posts too close,
after all, to be much use either.   So

motion supplies us, an eager genie, with
the unity we crave, and the rock whose beat
attunes so readily to the rhythm that the
joins in the surface create beneath the wheels
of this vehicle which disguises from the inhabitants
in each new center our own newness, how we come

in the known way of prophets and other
disrupters of the public calm, incognito,
three strangers no doubt but there, right
outside the diner, the chevvy that serves
to guarantee we are sufficiently like them
to constitute no threat.   Nothing untoward

about our orders, and how could there be? The menu
takes care of that.   Mildly offensive in citified
clothes and the speed of our speech, we will be
gone within the hour, even our slight
exoticness familiar, out here where destinations
are as vague as they are polarized.   Since this is

only the second day of the trip, too soon yet
to miss the parking problems of our particular
four-block homeland, and still not used to the fact
that the phone cannot be ringing for us, we indulge
in fantasies of settling here, someday, we could
buy this joint, renovate a white frame house, raise

chickens or marijuana, slow down our heart-rates,
let little Fran experience clean air and older
values, become somebody to be nodded at or
conversed with, an exchange with plenty of spaces
in it for good fellowship to ooze its way into,
let the world go to hell in a handcart, we'll bring

plenty of videotapes and snap up bargains
in antiques, live like forgotten lords.   All these
inventions upon the theme of what we've just been
briefly among we save, of course, until on the road
once more, after the doors have slammed against
the outside and the quaint, threatening talent

that might take exception to a banter having them
for its occasion, not knowing it is kindly meant.
Hundreds of miles to go before we sleep (try sleep)
in some Oceanview Motel with its door habitually
chained and its exhausted appliances.   Ah! the camera
is, you see, safely with us, still.   Snapshots—

her before a bank of wild orange poppies, child
blurring at the final instant; him
daring the steps of a cove-side cliff—
later will mean their interstices too,

each dozen or so yards caught for the head to store
in its inexhaustible circuitry, where the view has been

automatically matched up with proprioceptive
sensations, assuring friends of various accounts
that this vacation, that evening after dinner, is going to
turn out to have been.   But something more,
which surely we share, is happening: something is
shifting, the way unimaginably giant plates

out of sight are always shifting, we are not only
told, but can't help noticing (these mountains here):
the map some of us studied before setting out
is unrolling itself into a physical experience,
making the isolation of origin and terminus
vanish, to be replaced by a lived continuum

that enhances our grasp of reality.   So,
even though we are part of a generation
close enough to the horse era to be slightly
self-mocking of such insulation as eight
cylinders and a brand-new set of tires provide, we,
unlike our compatriots who do it by air in two hours,

do enjoy the privilege of discovering just
how it does all fit together.   The landscape,
eventually, does change, massed conifers
replace the bare sweep of grassland, while,
glimpsed from each bridge, the rivers
have white in them now, and the highway, many more,

and sharper, twists.   Then this in its turn
yields to fertile farmlands, to fail,
sometime next day, in their turn, before the encroachments
of used-car lots and motels that say "City
coming up".   We feel like politicians,
able to speak superficially to its denizens

concerning the environs intent upon their center.
We may not know it, but, voted for, by jimminy,
we could begin to learn.   And, face it,
if one will only overlook their provincialisms,
the scarcely warranted pride in the downtown
renovation project, the exorbitant praise or

condemnation of the tarted-up ex-warehouse
neighborhood with its prawn-bars and Victorian
street-lamps, they are, this people, much like us.
Obvious meliorists, transparently hopeful of being
liked and accepted, prickly withal
in the presence of the slightest condescension,

eager to display their currency
under the spreading yellow of the latest issue.
Here, just as at home, a friend—he has been
contemplating this meeting for days, weeks, on
and off, with a mixture of sophomore yearning and adult
distaste for the excessive—alters all,

as a three-dimensional figure, although only on film,
causes its cartoon companions to become at once
jerkier and flatter; and a miracle occurs,
right there, on his front lawn, as this man, that
one of us, more years ago than we care to mention
(but we do, we do), sat up with night after night

drinking his old man's Canadian Club, throws his arms
around the body of his erstwhile buddy
for the first time in their lives.
And here his wife comes, dimpling, excited,
having heard so much about us . . . . it's altogether
too much too soon, given the hours cooped up

together in our space capsule, speaking to no-one
except deskclerks and waitresses.   But what's this?
A drink has been socked into one's hand.   Good,
very prescient of society to have thought of it.

Deep sighs.   When all's said and done, and barring
having a 12-gauge shotgun thrust through the rolled-down

window at that drive-in, POW-EE!
or (and face it, a much likelier inter-
ruption) getting a blowout fifty miles from the closest
phone, nothing thus far could be said to have
prepared us for this reunion, the first time,
this trip, when things might get out of control.

For he seems, doesn't he? somewhat
odd.   Has he altered as much inside
as on his (distressingly aged) surface?
Is he about to run some numbers, feeling
(a) superior, or, (b), inferior
but anxious therefore to deny it?

Is his female visitor prettier
(to his view of it) than his wife?
Or does he simply envy his guests the
(really, quite monotonous) expedition which,
all along (and can't he see this?) had him
as its object? Maybe that embarrasses? One thing

for sure, he's drinking too much.   And his guests—
can't he see how they're suddenly
inexpressibly weary, need to lie down, stretch out?
No—don't tell me!—he's taking out his
banjo!! He means for everyone to sit up singing
those dumb songs we used to sing all night!

Another drink? It could almost be done—but
little Fran is running dizzy circles
that arc so close to all their frangibles it won't be
long until—"Never mind, no, really,
it doesn't matter, that old thing!" Arabella
has a tight top lip but keeps on smiling.   She knew,

just knew, it would turn out just like this.
Nor is Penny any more supportive, forced herself
to witness a calculated risk come home to roost.
Men, why do you make women your reality testers,
litmus paper to your unexamined hopes? Penny
studied Hegel, Kant and Heidegger, her dissertation

relates ethics to esthetics, she works long hours
with underprivileged persons in the inner city,
wants to spend the rest of this week
lying on the beach. "Copasetic" was the word
used over and over to persuade her the expense of a hotel
would not be necessary, because these people, Tom and

Arabella, this very moment being vehement as it were
in private, just across the room, would be totally
undemanding hosts. A hotel will be located
in the morning. No big deal. The Bankamericard
checks will need to be larger for the next few months,
is all. Some small luxuries, even maybe a few

necessities, impossible from here to know just which,
will have to be forgone. That's life. A slight
awkwardness at breakfast, seeing there's no way
not to construe this alteration in our plans
as a rejection—either of their persons or their
property, or both—imparts a manic animation that

can't go on forever: so off, away! with promises
to meet for dinner later in the week. The hotel is
marvelously spacious, great light, looks right
down on the beach where slow days pass,
shlepping about in thongs, fingering small stones
and shells, buying knick-knacks, kicking back,

scribbling postcards to all the friends
we wish were here. Fran's delight at the waves
lulls her anxiety (why here, and where are we, and will we
never go back home, and when) throughout the day,

but it surfaces in nightmares and her shrieks
(they'll think we're killing her!) only subside

when she's fetched into her Mommy and her Daddy's bed.
Not much opportunity for love-making—Penny lying
warm and tender breathing next to her husband in the dark,
or suddenly revealed, taking off her swimsuit, sunlight
silvering her downy skin, shadowing the still-firm
musculature of her thighs and belly: like a distant

whisper urging to some action—but Fran's
giving up naps, and the unmistakable lovers on the beach
hone the word wistful to a blade.   Trumpets, electric
fender riffs! Remember when we did it
behind a driftwood log? Think what use we'd once have put
this king-size bed to, the sun-spread carpet too! Sobbing

cellos.   Well, the food is good, and the dinner
with Tom and Arabella (their kids are sitting Fran)
goes better than was feared, with everybody
remembering to act like strangers that a long sea-voyage
has thrown together, *tres gai*, Penny with her fresh
tan and a summer frock's a knockout, and there's

pretty good champagne, and everyone makes certain
each of the others has a chance to talk
about his or her work, once the latest tv shows and movies
(and, less promising a topic, books) have been
presented.   The day of departure dawns.   The two men,
lunching together.   Tom drinks too much again and drops his

bombshell: "What gives with you—you
used to have some guts!" Pressing right ahead
along memory lane, he names an art-hoax
that made the front page of the downtown paper
in their college days, links this up with society
hostesses insulted, expensive furniture dismembered,

some public nakedness, the marquee of the art-theater
tampered with until it spelled RAY ATE MARIE BAD—
incidents, he doesn't seem to comprehend, of a voice
wailing for a moral system to come
modulate its stridencies.   "This wife's no good
for you." Is he going to go too far? "She's great—

but not for you." That can be entertained. "Success
undid you." Here he's patently off-base; there has been
no success; the inventions that were to usher in an era
of universal leisure never jelled; and only one
product has made it to the market, a device
to prevent toilet-tanks from trickling; these days,

consulting for a company whose air-conditioning the
Pentagon approves of eats up all the time.   "You've lost
touch with who you really are." He means the chum
who urged him to make long-distance calls on the Dean's
phone to the harbormaster at Hong Kong.   Pathetically,
at last.   "I believed in you. " Repeated.   Helped to his

car, he vanishes in traffic.   Long-gone Tom.
Now the landscape is unrolling in reverse.   Penny's
profile enthralls as it has always had the power to—
power ceded to her, placed there by the man beside her
to be sure, yet, for him, emanating from her person, her
precise mix of yielding and resistance, pictured,

sculpted, there, the person courted and fought against
these seven years, this second marriage for each a long
balancing performance with little help from the so-called
community, desolate weeks apart or barely able to
endure a forced propinquity, murderous intensities,
sweet, sweet intensities, spells of sweet calm

and clarity of understanding shared—all this,
a mistake? The movie of it rounds the sprockets
all the way from days with Tom and Peg and Peter
and the gang, the places where it's been re-edited

as bits of gossip about who Peg really went through
her abortion for (not guilty me) came in: each move, if not

correct, then such as renders the notion of correctness
laughable, it was the only move, each time, to make,
given the tilt of the roadbed, the moment's
inertia.   And the enigma round the bend, all
each withheld.   Still, this is a silent stretch
of farm then forest.   We can't be who we are to

others if they lack accurate information about us.
Yet who doesn't? This isn't the wrong route, yet
could be, hypothetically.   The wise man didn't
come up with his formulation—"What we depart from
is not the way"—without strong provocation from
within.   And true enough, Tom, all was to be

revised, so little has been.   "The terrible
slowness of things"—Professor Conroy's intonation
of Matthew Arnold's phrase lives in his student's
recollection, as does the uprush of determination,
that first time it was heard, to speed things up.
A sign advises to conserve our gasoline.   Oneself,

then, alone, has been the proving ground, scant
consolation, ivory bourgeois inwardness copout.
Driving back across the open range, high summer
heat, shirt off, left elbow out the open window
the way the farmboys did (and do?) "back home",
Penny's man is flattered that she takes his picture

—she likes the look of him and means to keep it.
At a diner (not the one stopped at before; some variance
is possible) Fran charms the waitress with her own
pugnacious version of her parents' aspects—yes,
Penny's loveliness and poise are coming through
as a presence wholly unimaginable ahead of the event

and becoming quite predictable, there
within the vulnerable happiness this
developmental stage preserves.   "She's gonna be
a real ten"—thank you, and think of the problems
that attitude will soon create.   Oh, the road's
too long, we will never get there.   Yet already

the arteries are thickening to the great
heated heart, one of whose cells the home-comers
greet with wild whoops of grateful relief upon
entering, so glad to be back
it must be (for this moment) the only reason for leaving
was to have this sensation! To see and touch and breathe

in these familiar rooms felt for this present
no, not new, but wholly.   Fran
scurries to her room to tell her dollies
all.   Penny flops herself down on the bed.
And among this stack of bills and CARTSORT
stuff may be the envelope long looked-for—never
actually expected—to sweep this all away.

Waiting for Anyone but Godot

David Bromige

The flower that
opens and fills
the room with
scent, the eye
with color, how
blessed to us
seem such lives!
Does one choose?
By this he meant
to question a life
spent fetching up
stuff from the basement.
Philosophy
is less important than
humanity who
hope against
hope, and these words
can actually be
said.   Am I waiting
because I know

the word, or a word
because waiting
is my referent?
No moment need be
dull or indifferent
for the compulsive
conviction is never
our own. Judas
betrays interesting
parallels. He asked
his father did he
think living life
on the brink in
unremitting
intensity meant
one attained to
truth? His father,
picking his phrases
carefully, replied
No, not in any
sense that would
privilege intensity;
simply that one might
thus learn the truth
of such living. Each
character meticulously
unpacks a wallop.
Writing cannot
frankly write without
the estrangement of a
square and empty room.
To plot
a climax is
a disappointment in
advance. To be
disputes the premise
to remain its living
disputant. We find we
are frightened when

applied to most
profound shortfalls.
The ordeal being not
much deeper than
a puddle we judge
by its content not
its shape and yet
unassignable to
whatever might make you
think "chill
from the wind of doom".
That slow magic trick
that leaves the glass
half-empty, half-full.
Honor driven by
romantic dream, heroes
to themselves rank
forms. Paradox
can be a device
for generating
details and their
articles. The fact
that nobody
departs and says
he does must prove
our haunted genius.
Kept pent's best
entertainment to
forget all that's
already happened,
absorbing cavalcade
of humanity on
the rack. Parade
your drill, the Bible
knows it all and knows
it knows it all, and
even knows how you
might feel concerning
that predicated trap.

An electronic
gnocchi maker.
All over people
struggle towards
dignity while the
pictures precede
the blue pencil or
the shears, seeing
more things. Don't
you often or ever
wonder where we are
being taken, yet
surely it's more
where are we going,
the economist
can tell us this
as surely as the
priest he has
replaced. Teleology
shapes dialog. Often
I can't decide quite
what is being said.
Life is a nightmare
metaphorically
speaking at those
times when one
has lost control
to larger figures of
significance. Yet
irritation plus
depression want
to announce the
coming of calamity.
Antecedents stimulate
his transcending
imitation. Astigmatic
eyes register abnormal
persons in
abnormal circumstance,

baffling comparisons
with dramatic
asides—a history
exists to tell us
why we needed to
replace the infantile
sotto-voce lament.
He desires to
deserve the attention
he is getting.   Everyone
was acting
like so many
Freudian rats as
supreme effort clinched
its right to be one
of the great triumphs
of the individual.
It is encouraging to be
able to see the
forbidden, or sometimes
keenly traumatic,
inducing a blind spot
where his mother
dipping him in the river.
This convincing thesis
does much to explain
pointless endings in
terms of failure to
find peace by natural
conscience or scientific
reason when
God and rejection
coincide.   An admirer
of faith in life
will invariably attempt
the dismissal of dismal
disillusion.   The diction
of inconsistent realism
reaches the obvious

conclusion that
there are no mistakes.
The man he had argued
this with is long
since dead because he
hanged himself.   This
jawbreaking endurance
contest containing
certain literary, perhaps
poetic qualities
took place at a party where
he thumped the cheese
board with his fist to
emphasize his point
and in one kind of movie
that he liked, it
would have split.
I want
this and that
but gladly settle
for this if
only I knew.
Like characters
on top of a wedding
cake, you kneel
before the holy
church, to offer
unattainable
vows of love, worrying
the statistics of
marital fate, but
one's intelligence
might bring it off,
a long shot, provided
you are flexible
enough to give
up the initial
ideals yet stalwart
and brawn enough to

hang in there and
accident of course
will enter such
considerations.
Gardens were conceived
of as orderly
distillations of
the natural world,
—a place they tended to
view as threatening and
chaotic, especially
at the wild fringes
of the expanding Empire.
From this xenophobia he stood
apart by postulating
Nature as its own
scheme of orderliness,
dangerous yes and a place too
of great puzzlement, yet
meriting keen exploration.
They wrote about hamlets,
the problem the reflective
mind can pose divorced
from effective action,
open-mouthed before the
spouting geyser.   His
sciatica had cleared
itself up this morning.
The constant
detaching of the artist
from earlier ideologies
in order that the people
may enjoy an immortality
at second hand
—"the time
seemed longer",
in an irrepresentable
continuum offering
latent pictorial

structures in
two places at once
like arithmetic.
Definition of
horological terms may
be awkward: they
represent
components of dynamic
devices which must be
seen to be believed.
On Thursday
we intend to drive
over the mountains
to the hot springs
and this is attractive
both due to the destination
and the deep
satisfaction obtained
from an intention
realized.   The globe's
weight drives
the measurement
of its own
motion. Being Saxon
she placed a bowl
with a hole in its
bottom into water
where it took a prescribed
amount of time to
sink. Simple outflow
limited the length
of senatorial
speechifying.   More
personally, as a child
I endured considerable
anguish—my mother
hated to make
plans and my father
made meticulous

itineraries which
created great
anxiety in him, now
responsible for their
execution under the
withering eye of his wife.
I started to read and write
early and kept at it—
I could space it all
out at the kitchen
table, head in text in
text in head in
text—nowadays
it is the principal
relief from my troubles,
which is why I choose
not to amuse you
with them—so much so
I must wonder whether
I am somehow maintaining
in my life a given level
of misery simply to keep
the writing need going—
Foxe's *Book of Martyrs*
was impressive, he kept
on praying while flames
that otherwise must have
hurt him horribly
went apparently unnoticed.
I spoke to her
without much
forethought, asking
if she had dreamed
and she replied "I
dreamed about the river
and the ocean" which is
her customary response to
that inquiry.   Time
to put on the water for

morning tea, I recalled,
so did, and then
had to think of something
to do that wouldn't
take very long as the water
boils almost at once
in the small saucepan.
To resume the novel found
so hilarious last night
might be to burn
the bottom out.
So I watched a segment
of "Sesame Street"
standing up.   You have to
remember to fill the cup
to the brim, because
once the teabags are
removed, the level is
bound to drop.   All this
time I kept right on
in- and ex-haling.
Only a contrast reveals
the distance
literal or metaphorical
that one has traveled.
The merits are almost
completely technical
infelicities.   An
impressive absence
of meaning invested
our desires.   T,
F. TGIF.   Comparing
something obviously
long with something
clearly short has
something of the
trick about it.   Critics
feel play bears.
Grand interlude for those

above average intelligence.
A portion of the iceberg
will shortly have
been specified. DNA
permits suggests
engenders this
spiralling
redundancy. Great
is the English
tongue. You can't
contradict the multitudes
you don't contain.
Theory
can't protract the moment
depended on by its
critique. He spots
the tops
of the posts
and stops. These
tones, the gray
stone wall gone
green with moss
and light reflected
from these great
green leaves, the greener
green the leaves
themselves surrender,
felt calm to him,
leaned against the
edge of the large
hot bath, and the steps
cut in the stone
were an obdurate
instance of one
self, approachable yet
resistant, holding
much in place
and letting change
settle in little

noiseless shiftings
while keeping
up a general appearance
of substantial
permanence.   Which
leaves to account for
the leaves themselves,
and the greater extent
of the branches of the
figs this spring
contrasted with the sure
recollection (knowledge!)
of this time
last year.   Secret
society 200 strong
seeks to engineer
lasting partnership
among the ruling
classes of the more
advanced industrial
nations, but encounters
resistance in the form
of mass hallucination
concerning the separation
of the political and
economic realms.   A mad
doctor tries to create
a race of supermen.
Horror rises from the tomb
to terrorize descendants
of decapitated French
knight.   Merry
lady-killer marries
young women for their
money; In Tahiti, a wild
bikini gets stuffed
into a shallow plot.
A consul plays Cupid
for a GI and fiancee.

Secretary weds boss to
protect him from women.
Stern railroad
superintendent reveals
his heart of gold.
The dollar
being strong
that summer, we
would have been dumb
indeed not to avail
ourselves of it.   Societies
like to suppose themselves
natural, all others
artificial.   Alternatives
challenge god-given
rights and persons
bringing these to mind
ought to be excluded
for the good of
the republic.   Patterns
of exposition repeat
other social patterns.
Of the one
hundred or so
varieties of apple
in America, Safeway
markets 4.   The texts
of which the teacher
received free samples
and which were calculated
to aid in the instruction
of students learning
composition tended to
repeat each other.
Marx makes capitalism
aware of itself as
human construct.
Now it has been
mostly destroyed we

really start
to appreciate the past,
the infinite and rich
variety of human
being we're obliterating
even as it passes into
a plethora of texts.
To study how
caste, class and power
develop in a village
in Tanjore not only
tells us of ourselves,
it also baffles
and bewilders, usefully
telling of our limits.
All's codified—is this
to keep one's cultural
heritage alive, or simply
to be extraordinary
in a document? Sift,
organize, then couch,
these steps we prize,
along with quantifying:
if good at same,
should qualify
for an elite,
the shroud
of that mystique.
The mountains are
many and rugged,
thickly populated
close to the edge
of hunger. Fetched
to the new world
to be slaves,
we mixed our blood
the better to
escape or to increase
our odds the way

one plays various
combinations at
the track.   What is
being born for
if not for this?
The Hamadsha
of Morocco slash
their heads,
entranced, during
their healing ceremonies,
in this highly
readable account.
Although the gods
destroyed the villages
the goddesses belonged
to, phallic figurines,
female perfection in
one handy symbol of
the masculine excrescence.
Madstone or mole,
birthmark to balmyard,
hope rendered concrete,
by this waterfall
their stand was made,
an amusing dissertation
concerning head-hunting.
Your executioners later
cower in terror
before your ghost.
Poker can be viewed
as a religion, unequal
parts of skill,
nerve, luck, distracting
the way to carve forms
in a rockface keeps the
carver from picturing
catastrophe he can't
keep in the rock.   Solid
nuggets of some

fascination. An
eliminated people
qualify under the
Dewey decimal
system. In the lowlands
bands of anomalous
Christ-worshipers—
in cities, intellectual
excitements—in Japan's
megalopoli, moxibustion
clinics, lock the cultural
thesis. An anonymous
Asia says, If you must
restrict your interest
to just one
book, try this. A husband
and a wife are laying
out the politics of
reproductive ritual,
stirring up something
new and lively, maybe
that better job affording
the offspring of their
union a better crack at
turning things around,
or leastways an education in
reframing. The Lacadones,
last lords of Palenque,
there in their mahogany
forest, beautiful,
remarkable, reduced to
250, wouldn't thank you
if you asked and could be
understood. In fact
isn't understanding,
save where it can be
demonstrated by use
of the tool, rather
a feeling or sensation

that one has understood?
Meanwhile in northern
Thailand, the interplay
between the structural
dominance of women, the
ideological dominance
of men, vividly
brought out, challenges
earlier perspectives.
The folktale, singing
for power one crazy
February evening
behind mud walls to
people without history
beneath the bo-tree
about art, results in
a picture triumphantly
impregnable. Sogdian
painting, with its
distinctive
traits, color plates
and many line
drawings, the psychology
of art is never simple,
not if the alphabet
can have its say—
the choice hardly
seems there to be
made. Giants
like Cezanne strive
to arrive at some
final grasp do they
of form as problem?
Color his rectangle
pink. Art has to be
seen in its religious
context and religion
in historical context
or what we term the

bottom line.   An immensely
likeable hero, a succinct
sound motion, careful
synthesis of documents
and technical
sources, *con amore*,
where seeing is
forgetting the name
of that you see—
the burning ambition,
the servicable cliche,
provincial naievite and
leapfrogging
inspiration, what
is the economic role
of government? I can't
recall since when,
but it seems forever,
this assumption that
I am the epitome
and the apotheosis, why
else live, and how?
Under the delusion that
the center is
elsewhere? The creative
personality makes use
of the art-ideology
his culture supplies—or,
an instrument the community
makes use of to express
its cultural ideology—
which he composes with
all the vigor of his
personality—the constant
detaching of the artist from
earlier ideologies,
corresponding to
a separation of
the individual

from a great
whole, and also
to the extrusion of
wornout ego parts in
a gesture of independence
that, hailed sufficiently
as a successful one, will
bring the dependency of
fame, the people (us)
needing someone to be
famous so we can
participate in his or her
immortality—success
a stimulus for just so long
as it is not attained:
I wonder who reads Otto
Rank these days? A strobe
lumped at a desk.   Patient
days of abstruse
thought.   Wants to be noted
as performing something
if not useful then
with the *gegenschein* of
purpose trailing it, who
so instructs that words
shall so appear and
form? Religious in
its unappeasibility,
the impulse struts
fanes, while bells
batter its erections,
while its solitary fellow
follows demonstrating
phrases such as
"sure of his welcome (here
at any rate)" and "individuality is
an epiphenomenon of late
bourgeois culture
astonishingly

persisting in this
era of recapitalization."
Which is not irony unless
a white shirt and a tie
are irony.   It felt
good and bad, beating that guy
out of a parking place
in front of the store
with the best xmas
cards in town.   Impediments
from day to day renewed put
paid to lofty hopes.   No
moon at all can be
a thrilling jazz number.
He figured the reason he
stole so much he was
he was looking for
a conscience.   Half
our nature's to
forget.   The movie
overlooks its
cameras.   Teenagers
manifest much
energy, it pours
into the sunset so
poignantly devoid of
another to appreciate
it with.   Even the red
barns with their white
trim meant sexual
excess.   Exogamous
longings for
someone with a trail
to be hot on, along
the echoing
chasm.   She hugged him
and then
thrust her belly up
to his and rubbed it

back and forth—
the past is
then anatomized
for all
imaginations, yet
at what cost in
distraction! Westminster

PIP

Maurice Scully

what was that
word that
first word that

trapped slick
head slow a
splash zone

around a gap
that might be
the –

roots wrapped
round a stone
reach down to
track –

the steps that
might be a
sound what was
that first((ripple))

that first
word a fabric
in the past
absorbed by

passing time may
be makes orb or
its coherence
yr memory my

chance our lives
together over
there hold still
now in the dark

what was it?

.

talking to
you noticing
something
strange

talking to
you listening
to what
we're

speaking
telling you
watching
you

listening
saying
noticing
something

a change
a beginning
a to each
retrodicting

differently
both each
noticing both
passing

the over-
lapping
regions of
preparation

& hoping to
shift an inch
or two
on –

plinth – clock –
time – a long way
back – &
so …

to begin the Osani
game the children
sit in a circle
feet touching

while each in
turn names
an object
that is round –

the sun, the moon,
an eye – continuing
to

figurative
expressions –
the family circle,
togetherness,

the lunar cycle
& so on
until players
fail to come up

with a term
that is 'circular'
& drop out.
tradition has it

that the last
remaining player
will live a long
& prosperous

life. a winner.
osani, the Congolese
pygmy word
for love.

A Tale of Two Cities

Ken Bolton

I wonder if Pete is at Self Preservation—his coffee shop—
much, these days?   He is, I guess, if it still does the job

—or will it have 'ceased to confer change, respite', become
the wallpaper, the ceiling you have, in his words "stared

too much at"? I like to think of Pete there.
I imagine clatter, his awareness of what goes on.

Am I so aware?
Not really.

The coffee here "is good"—tho not as good as Peter's.

I should probably just 'Ask For It Stronger'.
Will I?

I'm glad I thought of reading him again, & came
to this solution—'faced it' even as a problem. Self preservation.

A small problem—but since I solve no other …

Where Pete sits—just inside near the door—on the black
divan or bench, *I* sit similarly, at the first table.

#

Tho in Adelaide   —   to his Melbourne

#

Aside from the two girls who serve,
there is not much going for it—I look at the street

because the interior is not sufficient, the customers not usually
        interesting,
to me.

#

                    There's
'nothing else', between here & work (the street
in a long despond).

                  The length of the walk
recommends it.

Even so, you get here: & then it's not enough.
I will abandon my coffee shop. When did I

last do that? Usually they fold, & *then* I make a choice.
I could move 'next door' (two doors down). Actually,

#

I don't like the street. (I could move : 'to a new side of town'.
As in the song.)

#

This is momentous. What was it
Lenin said — "What is to be done"?

What was that song Lenin sang?

When he sang that song —
what did he sing?

The two Korean women who serve here are very nice

An even further walk is the *Boulevarde*. I could go there—
forget the coffee!—& be in touch with *life*—a fugitive

from my class & kind, *a spy in the house of*
nuts,

whom I have known—
to nod to now, various of them, for decades

some acknowledge me, some don't—thinking, in all likelihood,
Who is *that nutter?* Or maybe they've just *cut their losses.* They see

a refugee, from his own class—who might
'repair there again'—at any time—a man

with no loyalties

a completely deracinated dreamer—compass marked
Ted Berrigan, Lou Reed, Karl Marx—(& some principles, probably, of
          my father's,

or Theodor Adorno—who *never met my dad*
whom

like the old guys at the *Boulevarde*
he'd have got on better with than me

that is, better with my father—no-one
gets along with them at the *Boulevarde*

#

This is the sudden withdrawal
Of All Good Will   …   for a realpolitik

of tooth & nail? What a day!)

#

did I mean, anyway, "declassé"? (I.e.,
not "deracinated"?)

#

he *might* have got on with my father better than I did

And what of Lou, Ted, Karl? Can Imaginary Friends
'turn'?

Where does that leave me?
The two Korean women.

#

They know my name—& I know theirs. They have never been
unkind to me. As far as I can tell.

I have never been mean to them.
Tho of course, *I am thinking of leaving.*

#

There are my *real* friends—Michael & Julie, but they are real,
& I am fooling.

#

I read some of the new stuff the groovier press put out—
groovier, but not that groovy—play Lou Reed—& cheer up

I am back on my feet again.
My mental feet.

#

**Romans cultivated the feet
& used its leaves as a vegetable**

the beet, the beet.

#

I will not read *that* poet again. "(M)y surging blood,
my reasoning mind". I read Ted. (I read "*again*, instead, Ted"!

My position being
So much for lyricism)

Some people prefer the internal monologue

And a crazyman taking hostages & shooting them
in the name of an idea, walks free, months after killing his wife

If our laws protected women—
as they protect men, from, say, king-hitting each other—

she might be alive. Along with the others. A patriarchal,
woman-fearing nation. Our is, theirs is. Here, Sydney, Adelaide—

Melbourne, Baghdad.

Ideas are to agree with, disagree with, assent to or discount.
If I hold a dumb one

it is my right—& the duty of others to point it out.

Respect others' ideas?—I respect their right to *hold* them.
But a dumb idea is a dumb idea. I mean,

"just quietly".

'Learn to duck'?

#

Can it really be religion? Not impatience with Imperialism,
the long durée of Western hegemony, Western disdain?

That is, economics & nationalism? But the world is strange—
evidently, & stranger than I had imagined.

I don't have a good feeling about it.

"There are problems in these times,
 But—woo-woo—none of them are mine!"

Lou, Lou, would that it were so.

from
like hypnotising chickens

Keith Jebb

like hypnotising chickens

push peoples' heads down reality
vision kills creativity comes
into focus Johnny inhaling
ceramic dust from tiny seeds
says 'I do a striptease I say
the text I boss the Somali fixer
I'm the will-gill take you up the
bum the arse the shitter the

turn. he says this. he's the people's
head I talk suck through no
aliens on this time-line push
Jimmy's head down Johnny the
plane's wanting left to Angola
passengers stare and they ride

ratio on the shotgun. no aliens.
I mess with the prerecordings

cut-and-splice history is now as
the president's pauses the little
deaths within each sentence
Blackwater running the show
as Xe (some chinese philosopher
cooked up by a CIA Poundian

because capitalism sees the
funny side just no smile no
giggle beyond the wet stretch
of cloth across your face
a serious operation on your
skin removes what lies beneath

is nothing you know what they
want. sticking the probe
up your anus with the style
of a martian poet shags
badgers behind the ha-has
of national trust lawns while
faber new poets sip bubbly
on the terrace not knowing

they're next. And Johnny
old queen saw it happen
realtime the 80s again
the oxbridge summers
under dripping awnings
smells of pimms leather and

dog the necessary fouling
the flagstones cracked weeds
breaking through skin of
the city the no society the me-
at-head the look green shoots
the. feeling a terrible nostalgia.
I'm all together in this paid
tax for the rhetoric I couldn't un

vote the big city skin of London
flapping around me cat-in-a-
wheelie bin culture clutching
a pole on the tube spitting
amongst the hissy-fits of i-pods
coming apart coming unstitched

he was there face an over
grown 12 year old little
smirk he can't wipe clean
the lurch for the doors
minding the gap we mind
full of the gap where 'some
thing happens' opening in
the skin I wriggle free from

small croc escapes holdall
back of the plane and every
body rushes forward and
only croc survives the crash
gets macheted by a
rescue worker who's bad

this is plyboard wings
strapped to arms
801 squadron flaps across
the carrier deck stealth sub
beached off Skye didn't
see itself coming 24 hr
rolling news coverage
sponsored by cobra

is my bad watching the light
fall into the thames glints
off canary wharf pyramid.
we'll build a new cardboard
city for the twenty-first
century. and we'll rent it.

Johnny's got a squat in
kilburn Johnny's got weak
verbs Johnny's got nobody no
body's got Johnny saw
fox running the underground
slipped off the platform
onto the tracks and trotting
at the tunnel's mouth and

silently away. fox died. just
smell of him now. just awk
ward questions the great
whiskers northern fox
gone to earth in the capital
never looks in the mirror.

my conspiracy
(for Kevin Doran)

of course it was me. and every
body else knew me so go figure.
you were the best and we
had plans for you. i had. i was the
massive white cyst or sac
bouncing along the shore at
your escape. i wanted information
and i got it. i drove you mad.

easy to say and hard to feel.
we work like chickens on our
egos. and i Johnny missed the
clues you bitch. the cargo cults.
how every writing was a glass
plate of your negative. a soul.

read all about it

this poem has tapped your phone.
this poem has been through your bins.
this poem has seen your medical records
and this poem is concerned for you.
this poem tapped up your brother-in-law
and an interested party in the Met and
this poem doesn't believe you when
you accuse this poem of intrusion be

cause this poem is good. this poem
has the perfect cover-up it has the
ear of the PM and all his friends and
enemies. this poem would not lie
to you. this poem has forgotten more
about you than you will ever find out.

johnnysong 4

i know where you live. i see you every
morning about your ablutions as they
used to say i got me under your skin.
and i will break out. i am an outbreak
of the mirror the razor close to where
ever you thought it was safe i am the
fleck of blood in the basin i am the
change in the mouth's geography i am

unaccountable. rot. decay. a
gradual loss of coherence a loss
of cohesion i am a loss of who
you think you are. forget this me you say
by from or out of. i have no face but
i am behind yours. i am that clumsy.

Phrases

Scott Thurston

PHRASE XVII

Are you here?

Hidden behind this surface where the god stares out?

My feelings presented a proud picture of eroticism stretched, taking over: clinging most strongly to what is weakest in me.

Imagined my feet in the other space.
A gesture of holding a volume away
from me whilst in a lunge.
The floor folded over a piece of language,

putting control outside. For what was
I late, if all I was after was my self? Could
it reinforce as well as release? We spoke
and danced each other's material.

Rest,
comforting of head,
enquiry of ear,
turning into oil.

Remembering how
I go through this,
deciding to accept
the rise into spring.

Language said no
deal: mouth said deal.
Intimacy which can't be

achieved under default conditions.

Integrate a bloc of postures,
wanting to see it unencumbered.

How to prepare for death,
ensure a safe transition?

How to make a new mark in space?

How to go from one step to another,
to take up a clear position?

We knew at certain points we would
meet. It didn't always happen.

Do you want to take me,
shatter my heart in two?

PHRASE XVIII
for Vicky Karkou

Hands straight out
    in front,
parallel to the floor,

in and out,
coming together,
    pushing out,
slanting side to side,
left to right,
    all in the hands,

the left cups the right,
hands held in front
    of the solar plexus.

Kneeling on floor
bending forward,
forehead on floor.

The right arm
fully-released.

Describing a small box
in front of the knees.

Shifting to one side,
evoking different relationships –
    holding it, lying down
next to it, turning away from it.

Describing two
arcs on the floor
    with the left hand to the left,
right hand to the right.

The right hand writing.

Reaching out to the box,
then coming in towards
the solar plexus.

Then end.

Rippling reaction
through body,
two hands
more controlled,

asking if one
missed the words.
Then hands conjoined –
struggling, fighting.

Move and throw
words in,

have words
and throw

moves in.

Slow down and repeat
when you move
with the reading.

PHRASE XIX

I don't desire romantic ruin:
but words must be unchained,
break against the grain

exposing the thought that was
not mine to put.
Short vowels announce

a dark theme:
poetry as accessory
to identity.

To really look death
in the mask;

to cross a bridge
in the rain, realising

I can't keep
pushing any more.

Losing focus in stillness,
getting too attached
to my projections.

Where I was who I was.

Spinning across the room,
the landscape shifted,
previous positions

dropped away.

Dancing in relief
at sharing the burden:
in a forest between
shape and sound,
point and rhythm.

So that it could be seen.

Do the dance
of sun
and moon:

impossible roster.

Looking at the floor,
if you can
look at a thought,
look out of it,
lock in to
a dead dock leaf
and see its life.

Follow the direction of a push to the hip. Shake off a mask, find it difficult to come back into the world.

In this phrase: be a politician of form.

Four Poems

Donald Wellman

What string cuts like an ice string?
Luminous blocks of blue ice
cut from the ice shelf.
On this surface a young priest
dances in seal skin leggings
polar bear cuffs at wrists and ankles.
What fish but the artic salmon
thrives in the waters of Kotzebue Sound?
Its red flesh flayed on the ice.

Donne and Eliot infiltrate
the fissures of my brain.
"Ash Wednesday," I argued
is not the act itself. Climbing
the narrow-gage stairs,
my foot slips on worn carpet.
Descending I fear falling.
No vistas here of cosmological gardens,
hedges cut in arabesques.
I approach where I hope to go
and crawl over the threshold.
In the rhapsodic pangs of suffering transport,
Donne begs God to ravage him.
Words and meditation
revolve in separate spaces.
The words outside like a storm of stars.
The interior dim to insensate fingers.

The body of a woman on a butcher's slab
could be his mother. Anger turns to sadness
without salvation. The face looks
like a map of Holland, in a time of aerial
bombardment, humanoid shapes
without noses, ooze like slime molds
on a dirt floor where children cling to mothers
and mothers know from the way heads
fall away without resistance that war has
come to an end. Their kids dead.

Where two tones approach
there's an edge before they meet
as when a hair falls
over a brow and it rises
on the breath. Two lungs catch
an insubstantial whisper
between worlds. So
I thought of how I wanted
to be disposed when
I had lost consciousness.
No intervention of tubes
to feed my failing form.
No paddles to shock
a heart, no longer mine.
Do not resuscitate! Monitor
the light in my eyes!
When that margin between feeling
and fading dawns, let me collapse!
The notes collide!

Ribbons

Michael Rothenberg

When I see ribbons in winter morning light
I know I haven't slept long enough

Seated at the kitchen table in the tropical cottage
Cup of Cuban coffee in my hand

Weary of the human condition
Notes will not be enough

Ribbons scream . . .

*

Hollywood, Florida

Three o'clock in the afternoon
Blue light streaks through frosted jalousie windows

The dog sleeps, wakes, listens, looks, barks, sleeps
I am lying in gloom suffering from a condition

Throbbing brow, aching eyes
There's no one here to set me free

*

Terri visits her mother down the street
She can't manage me any longer

She wants me to take a terrible walk
With the dogs but I don't want to go

Anywhere. I want to drift through
The shadowy bedroom ether

Of this Florida afternoon. Numb
Myself with wine and pills, imagine

Baudelaire (borderlands) and Henry Miller
Exhausted senses, wild visions

Timelessness, days without dates
(Deities) or meaning. Afternoons

without purpose (Affirmations)
I want to drown in the quicksand

Of sensuality with nothing to win
Nothing to gain and no one to torture

*

So I'm going home now
Dialing the phone number of the house

I once lived in 50 years ago
It rings through to an electronic nowhere land

Going nowhere. Just ringing, ringing
Back to my mother's voice

Or in this case to the housekeeper
"Rothenberg's residence"

Is my mother there, Ophelia?
"No Michael, she's not home anymore"

Again, every once in a while when I panic
I can't help but reach for the telephone

I find myself calling my childhood home
Ringing, ringing to nowhere

"There is no connection"
I figured that out one drunken night in 1984

(Wrapped in fog). No matter where I am
There is no connection.

                    January 7, 2014

Robbed

Joseph McElroy

This is not yet the story of my life though another fearless beginning
as fresh as I deserve. Visited by who I must be, with a thread of the
unknown and getting even and not only unpleasantness but the urge
to set something straight. I had learned I might find the man himself
in the general vicinity of the river walk. Old now and mysterious,
but all there and quite famous though private as could be. We had
lived in this exploding neighborhood for years without knowing one
another. Often away, both of us, and he, except for one moment
worth recalling, maybe two, had no reason to know the likes of me.

  I knew him at once, this seventy-something figure who
was sitting in a bench facing the North River and its vast activity
all before him and his walker. Knew him though I'm behind him —
standing room, call it. A rare picture in the paper once upon a time,
a recent shot in profile taken with a group — for all I knew I'd been
looking for him for years; but no.

  Nearby at the rail spitting down into the riverwash, two
young thugs, as we now loosely say, I did know; one of them
anyway, Thewy he was often called and a few other things, since
he was four or five running around in the park a few blocks from
here unsupervised. And I knew also that these kids, more than

kids, who would not know who this old guy with a small patch of
bandage on the back of his head was might mean him no good, and
maybe this was why I had come upon him where he sat, for how do
things happen, I've been trying to understand all over again. Ask
the visitors taking pictures out on the new spaces of grass where
people lay or picnicked and the walks and the bike path who knew
nothing of what had been here scarcely thirty years ago. In their
windbreakers and sneakers sharing their guide books, looking up
from their little maps, how would they know? They are the scene too,
passing through. This reinvented lower Manhattan, and right here
fancy views from some of these buildings built on landfill waiting
for the high-income tremors, maybe the first real earthquake in a
century and a half.

New Jersey waterfront across the River cleaned up and
hollow as the big clock which is better seen at night, and off to my
left the inner harbor where this supposedly great estuary meets
another, the East River, in sight of the sea or anyway the bridge
built almost in my lifetime to take the measure of The Narrows and
I would never say in *spite* of me. Two white commuter ferries were
crossing and between their wakes a seagoing barge and its tugs
ploughing the depth and roll of the current with a coastwise cargo
likely bound south. I felt for them in motion. Swimming the exercise
for me at the moment, which had been not bitter but a turning point,
and now I set eyes on this man whose birthdate put him at 76 and I
realized I'd been wanting to speak to him.

"AC ..." I said. A look of surprise and hope in his broad,
fleshy, austere face close up and squinting at me as I came around
the end of the bench; such attention and experience what you'd
expect from him, all he had found to show through his cameras for
forty or fifty years. He blinked perhaps against the light, his eyes had
their own way of seeing. A man, that was all, and looking into things.
"I know you. I think we've met," he said. He was a celebrity of a kind.

I sat down stiffly, a look down the rail at Thewy and the other
one. No, we had not met, at least I didn't think so; but I knew him —
"You do" — and had admired the documentary about Greensill, I
didn't know how he had done that. "Yes," he said.

Here I was, talking to AC. "How are you?" I said, like a fool.
"Moving," he said; "between apartments." "It doesn't look like it," I
said. Maybe he would need some help. Could be. "It's a mess over

there, a regular treasure hunt." I told him my name, his handshake was soft like a martial artist's I knew, not like an out-of-town *New Yorker* writer I had met who gave you two fingers.

The boys were nearer now, Thewy very street-strong, the blond buzz cut, the bones of his face unyielding; his friend deep olive, small and dangerous, listening, the eyes everywhere yet cast down. "Lucky you don't need one of these," AC touched a grip of the walker; "you're still young but when you sat down … ?"

AC sized you up, he got what he wanted, I must never forget that. My hip a long story short not worth getting into, crossing one leg over the other could throw me out of joint at this stage. "I saw you —" I said. "Right." "— and thought, *Greensill.*" "Ah, *Greensill.*" "The film *and* the man," I said, and swallowed. "No one remembers it," said AC. "But me," I said.

AC looked at his watch, rudely it seemed. "Not only you," he said. He hadn't seen me here. No, I worked for a living. To tell the truth, a former — (AC looked at me) — a former friend frankly had told me AC had been seen sitting down by the River — the filmmaker, did I remember? "Can't escape yourself," were AC's words, and I would remember and write them down. Was he still working?

"Trying to automate it" — a joke, but not a joke. In some mysterious way exact. He nodded, noncommittal, agreeing with himself. He guessed he would call it a day. He looked around him. A small sloop, its sails full, came about and bent toward us maybe seventy yards offshore. And now bearing down on a beautiful collision course above us, it turned again, a bearded man at the mast waving and a woman at the tiller though now standing in the well bending over doing something, and I was waving back when AC raised both arms and it was him they were greeting, the hull almost even with us now as if to hang very unsteadily on the shore swell — for a moment as close to the railing as the mainsheet flapping was palpable.

But look at Thewy, a great sight vaulting the rail to stand on one foot leaning out over the water from the narrow concrete ledge one-handing the rail to reach and shake hands, and do what? — pull the whole boat in or himself aboard? — a risk that he could fall between. "Thewy!" — his name my word for all I couldn't say or didn't know — "Join the Navy," I called, a job for Thewy, for it occurred to me we must find what is our job — while the burnished yachtsman at the mast amidships spoke to him, sort of shook hands and let go, a European accent I heard, he greeted AC; and the woman, who I thought I recognized, a musician, tossed a plastic-bagged fish at us sort of shockingly, it slapped the seat of the walker and fell to the pavement, a several-pound striper, fresh out of a pail, astonishing.

Thewy drew back, self-conscious, could have fallen in; he did a barrel roll back over the rail and was beside his friend, and over his shoulder said, "I saw yo wife," those were his words, astonishing. The first he had spoken to me in years, knowing many things but no longer my family; AC was standing right beside me.

AC asked would I pick up the fish. He waved to the sloop downwind downriver. Said he was calling it a day, had to get home. Thewy was discussing the adventure with his friend, the two of them leaning on the rail, self-employed citizens. "They would have taken you aboard," I called. The friend seemed to snarl at me over his shoulder, and then the boat was gone somehow on a brief reach out into the River, *ARMADA* out of Gloucester, MA.

AC spread a newspaper on the bench, I was holding in two hands the great silvery striped bass, a gob of blood at the gills "fresh and crisp," as the poet says. I said I thought they spawned in Rhode Island and some of them wind up here. AC said the kitchen could deal with it; "assisted living," he grinned. It looked big enough for a party of four, I said. I gave him a droll look. The new place a new brick apartment building you could see from here.

"These guys —" I lowered my voice, they were about to pass behind us — in the corner of my eye Thewy's jaunty walk, and his lieutenant's in step behind him — "I know them," I said.

AC wrapped the plastic-bagged fish in newspaper. "They seem to hang around," he said. "They're thugs," I said. "Can you imagine I've known Thewy since he was a toddler — he was probably never a toddler; early days, my daughter growing up," I swept my hand out behind us.

"I spoke to them," said AC, "but I don't think they believed me. Why should they?" "What did you tell them?" "Said I'd put them in my next film."

"As what?"

The question stopped AC. He had placed the fish in the

basket of the walker. "Raising money's the crusher. You know that as well as I do."

"Even you?" I said. I wondered why he would think I'd know.

"Right now I'm moving," AC took it away from me. Between two places, it was crazy. He eyebrowed Thewy and his friend at the rail. "You know them," AC lowered his voice, hanging onto the walker and sitting down again. "Let's see," I said, "I do and I don't" — ready to take the story further — Thewy at five or six a borrower of my daughter's scooters, visiting from group to group, working the park, not this one. At twelve an expert in his way, and on his way, strangely tolerated by the Precinct where his absent father had friends. Twenty-four now, I reckoned. Alert, maybe not listening to what two older guys were saying just within range, you didn't know. A gangster maybe making a living on his cell. How long would he last? Who had ever told him what he ought to do? I thought what was sort of eating me sitting here with this director who'd had an Academy Award, I remembered, or a nomination, one of the founders of a style, who'd stayed faithful to documentary which included not having been heard from in a while.

And the loft? "Oh it's no secret. It's over on Franklin Street," AC mentioned the address, "I've been there since JFK was President." I shook my head but I knew. I remembered the documentary about Eleanor Roosevelt's friend and how the two women walked, long-legged, wonderful. AC seemed to enjoy talking to me. "Now it's Senior Living with a wine list five minutes right over here."

Had he sold the loft? Hadn't moved half his stuff out, nowhere to put it. "The new place is ..." He shrugged.

I smelled the River, the sea, an oil slick.

"I danced once right over here," I pointed.

"At midnight with a damsel, music, champagne, the River?" said AC.

"Just the River. It was up aways. Before this existed." I pointed to the pavement. "Below here, where it was landfill beach in 1982, all of this, and I suppose still is; it may come in handy again, the beach. All these buildings rest on landfill, yours too."

"A pioneer," AC eyed me, a word from those days. "Just a dancer," I said. "No, I don't think so," said AC. A turning point. Excited, I nearly named the person I had danced with, but she didn't deserve it, and he didn't either. He was on his feet again, one hand on the walker. "I have a bone to pick with you," I said. "You don't say," AC looked down at me concerned that I hadn't told him. Maybe he could do something about it, you can always do something about it. But no, I was imagining things, clutched for words. "I like to know," he said; "like these kids, these thugs you call them — talk to them, they talk to you." True?, I wondered. He was a shrewd genius probably. Was he this open? "Out with it," AC said.

"Well," I said, "we had a deal with you. To film the company – modern dance company?" "Ah, this was in the Eighties," the great man looked down into my eyes; "trying to remember you."

"I had to be on the West Coast for two, three weeks, and when I came back the deal had died a natural death."

And by then AC was in Salt Lake City filming a ballet company instead. "Well, you know how that turned out." "They always have the money," I said. "It wasn't really about ballet, was it," AC said; "and more than Mormon money, the sensational press, the last throes of polygamy, all about *farming* —"

"Irrigation!" We laughed.

"But ballet," said the man. "How did you get those overhead shots?" "The cameras had some fun," AC rolled his eyes.

"Not that *we* didn't document *our* work, but this would have been something," I said. "We got some footage of you," AC said. "I wasn't there yet," I said. "The company," AC said.

"But I've seen some of it." "I think it helped you," AC said. "The company?" "You. Why do I think that?" said AC. "Things were never the same after that," I said. "Ah well, you're doing OK," AC said; "there's a lot left to do. Putting two and two together, Miller," he said my name. "You said the beach could come in handy again? You're an interesting person."

The boys were outa here, and AC called to them, "Your time will come." Thewy smirked at his accomplice and tossed a grin over his shoulder blade at AC. Tough thug with a buzz cut. What was going on? Did I guess? They walked single file.

I spoke of Greensill, my eardrums pounding, walking a Dakota flood on personal-designed pontoons, his wireless half-mile hailer addressing the multitude; lighting a fire on an Allegheny canal that had just been cleaned up — what the film had captured was Greensill himself off the cuff, troubled, alone, thoughtful, not thrilled, he'd offended almost everyone, and it almost went out of my head when I had said all this. "We would do anything to get what we wanted on film," AC said. He meant he would. AC released the brake of his walker, pushed the far handle to negotiate a left turn, which I could only watch, and then, his eyes on the horizon, reached his hand for me to shake, without looking at me, made his way around the bench and was headed home. "Greensill didn't believe in channeled rivers, but you know that, but didn't believe in us either," AC added over his shoulder then. "It was the planet. But you know that — someone like you, Miller — that your first name?"

Like *me*? "I'm writing now, learning the names of things, AC." He stopped a moment. "Anyway ...," his voice trailed off. Something told me he was not done. He trudged on with the walker beyond my wish to answer him, his last word. The new brick apartment buildings had prime views of the River. I felt my new hip joint speak, not asking to move as I once had moved and might again, but speaking only to me. I could write it down. Teaching me what not to like about this AC that had been at the ready in me all along and looking into things, if dance wouldn't do it.

Anna, I thought — the discolored sand just before dusk, we were not alone in the divisions and surprises of the dance we had made up, reading each other, seeming alike — words of a song say, "*Two* silhou*ettes* ..." words in my head say, *Two become one*, but those are words — while we closed in, darted slowly apart, thinking with our hips, our legs, lifting your leg with your two hands, drawing with arms and turnings, profiles and parallels such space between us performing on that lower Manhattan North River beach as to arrive at the feet of the small invited audience like fingers of tide just the two of us in the lowering light and the fairly pretentious but classical music from a boom box we were equal to, we were professionals, it was good work, a Downtown event in the early Eighties almost about this neighborhood whose sudden changes we could not own.

Anna's voice a little distant phoning one evening from New York to say we could forget about the film, as if to say don't hurry home; months later Anna herself in California calling here when it was three hours earlier on the Coast, for money; Anna in Chicago putting our daughter on as if Anna herself didn't want to speak to me; Anna momentarily at an unknown distance which proved to be a few blocks away right here in New York, sounding naked on the phone of a mutual friend last year.

Not unwilling to accept my company a second day at the River, AC wore a long-billed fisherman's cap this time. It started to rain and he showed no interest in seeking cover. It was voices we were talking about today, AC and I, I had told him Greensill *talking* (and partly in a foreign language) was as good as the unreal sequence of the dam cracking in an earthquake in Asia Minor or floods altering the course of a great Asian river, my former wife and I had seen the film together.

For I had looked at my notebook and found what I'd said yesterday and just on top of it the 212 number Anna had phoned me from which had not deeply affected me though it had given me a piece of information I would act on.

AC said, "Real talk has been replaced by trash."

"Trash talk? Haven't you done it yourself?"

"I'm doing it right now." A long hoot came from the harbor and a second and a third but more like city coincidences than answers.

"That's not trash talk," I said. AC was at the edge of the bench, not clear what he intended. I was after him now, just a city intimation, and instead of looking around me I took a pen and wrote down what had been said. "I'm not what I was, I'm far from it," AC said — what was it today? he said, meaning what had I written down? I looked up. "You just got people to talk, that's all it was," I said, "and you knew how to cut. Or someone did." He had a few things up his sleeve, I said. Ideas, said AC bleakly. "Still," I said. He had a strong constitution, a strain of gifted meanness.

AC gestured toward Thewy and his dark associate, with us again today. But they were leaving, they were walking single file away from the river and into the adjacent small new park. Thewy turned, like George Washington surveying the river walk or even us. Something's up, I said. *Up*, AC said.

I meant the boys but I could almost have not heard what came next from AC, seeing coming from the other direction, Anna. Thousands of miles from me and awful years not just years and maybe just a phone call away: today a woman my age. For it was she, in town always without warning for a night or three, who had called yesterday morning and in the course of a slightly off conversation told me that, in case I was interested, AC — remember him? — she understood was in the habit of sitting by the North River during the day, he'd had a fall and split open the back of his head.

Yet it was not the bandage that had struck me or especially identified him as AC yesterday, it was everything about him, it came to me; and anyway the bandage was gone today, leaving visible no more than a small shaved spot in the midst of his bushy, spiky gray hair. Surprised by Anna approaching, I was more struck by what the great man staring straight ahead at the River had said: "I may need your help over at the other place." "No problem," I said, his experienced eye upon the River, the wind, and focused now, I realized, on a pair of imperiled kayaks two hundred yards out like skateboards in a half-pipe.

Nor did he turn at Anna's voice, which once had meant to me my child, my home, my promise I will say, nights, food, uncanny jokes and beautiful slang, flesh and bones, dance and good sense and love.

And, once, betrayal. More than once. It was my name, its shortening, "Mill," that she, coming to meet me, pronounced thrice — yes, as differently as our dance vocabulary once could vary a bend, a lift, a pass through each other like particles, a full twist reaching for the ground or each other as the diver, for Anna had been a competitive diver and quite tall for it, and the unknown and unknown dive itself find the water with barely a splash. So that getting up and going behind the bench to greet her, feeling it in my back and my head, I could have found her legs and breasts real in the perfect timing of her kiss. But did not.

As she would know, but couldn't quite; and before she said what she had come to say, she called, "Thewy, Thewy, is it Thewy?" — (for there he was) — "You 'member me? Penny's mom? I'd know you anywhere, Mr. ThruWay." The other names, the early-scrapped given name Truex buried in a birth certificate like the surname, leaving him Thewy of Whatever — TriBeCa or the Wars or the Hood. He and his partner stood their ground. And AC, turning a quarter way around uncomfortably, seemed to meet Anna's smile leaning near him, as if he were unsure what was going on.

"Greensill!" Anna patted AC on the shoulder. "Wouldn't have recognized him," she murmured to me, and taking my hand,

said, "Hey, we could get married again," and laughed at herself outrageously. "How are you?" she said and was close and for a moment swaying. We heard AC make a sound and I saw one of the kayaks all but upside down. "I'm busy tonight and tomorrow," I said.

"And the day after that," Anna said.

"That's right."

She was meeting someone. She said she would call. I asked AC what he had over there at the loft and when did he want me.

Books, you know, books, and more books, the written word. (Anna was gone.) Boxes packed, and some going into storage needed to be consolidated. Bureau, chairs, tables maybe given away? Archives coming over here to the new place. Moral support, AC said. Day after tomorrow, he would take a cab and meet me there. The boys at the rail again were shoving each other. We discussed the kayak disappearing and then righting itself.

"Why me?" I said. AC gave me keys. So there was evidently no one over there.

"Did she go?" AC said, the boys at the rail listening I could tell. He knew who it was, I said. "Once I could have killed her," I said.

"You're frank."

"Humble her, you know."

"That all?"

I had thought it began way back, I almost didn't know when. AC was interested. She had predicted what would eventually happen to me. "I wanted to silence her before the predictions came true." "This was professional?" "And medical, almost the same thing. One thing after another. She said I was done long before I was."

AC said he remembered something to that effect. Experience of some parallel world, it seemed to me, probably kicking in for him. Well, he was inventive.

Twenty-four hours early I opened the Franklin Street street door and walked up to the third floor. They had installed an elevator some years ago in this loft building, but my two keys did not know the elevator.

At AC's door the longtime lock — only one — looked OK when it opened in one turn, but not the two turns it took when you turned the key full in, full out. Looming strangely when I switched on a bank of overhead lights, the ten-foot paint-gobbed wooden ladder standing open near a corner of the remarkably long, lived-in but not at present quite liveable space I at once climbed step by step I think to get free of cartons and furniture, freestanding bookcases and litters of possessions, stacks of photographs held together by rubber bands, to view what was really here. Some history or substitute I sensed, though events belonging not to one place or emotion or another, and up here the uneven surfaces of the ceiling had been painted and plastered not all at the same time, BX cable up the walls here and there ceiling-high and at two corners ending nowhere now. Something I missed. Even the ceiling in the dimensional vistas or blank freedom of its own spaces was not empty even of its own emptiness, and I did not want to stay up here or go back down to describe whatever paths I could find from one end to the other, an exposed kitchen unit of fridge and range in the distance in need of cleaning and of people, by another route a black sewing machine to trip over, beautiful with gold lettering, and altogether largesse of more than one life for a limping scrivener to record.

There was a dark, apparently smaller room off this one from which I was certain an odor of banana and perfume reached me where I stood on the eighth or ninth rung of my unsteady outlook. I was afraid, I will say; but, to the other room where the shadowy foot of a bed was visible, I was alert with a readiness that was all I needed and beyond the anxiety, the irritation I realized I had brought with me, for I found again reason to abandon what had abandoned me. Which maybe wasn't the way to go.

Our life is a failure but held together by an obstacle course of beginnings. Not words I shared with AC when we met at the elevator the following midday. Tough old man without his walker. And at first, to my surprise, his place apparently without the towering and suspect ladder I had stood on, when he flipped on the lights. It was not where I had left it. It was nowhere to be seen until I had a look in the adjoining room, dark and largely cleared, but for the bed. "This is quite some old ladder," I said. It was folded up and lying against the wall now.

"Can you beat that!" I heard AC say. "Damn. Damn. Damn. How about that!" his voice and now slow steps approaching at that special distance of the old days, those lower Manhattan loft spaces of the 1970s and very early 80s from the previous century, not exactly an echo but a sound miscellaneous of new arrival, or work, often unlicensed, going on, lonely and possible, free — just before word processors exploded into our lives. AC pushed past me into the room where I'd found the ladder folded together on the floor, and found the light switch. "Well they didn't take these," he said looking up. "These they left." Two surveillance cam units angled in opposite corners. "Have to see what we caught on this one."

AC using that old ladder was hard to visualize. I went and looked again at the long ceiling of the main space. I had seen yesterday two places where BX had been cut at the top, but the cams I thought would be battery-op.

I rejoined AC in the bedroom. As what? Someone he had once fucked over when I was out of town?

It had its droll side. "Did they take what you were trying to catch them with?" I said. "Catch them?" He was trying to find his cigarettes, I could tell. "Project I'm getting off the ground." He looked at me. He saw me as a real person, I think. The heck with my former wife.

Didn't the tapes get transmitted to a central office? Not these. "I guess Thewy and his friend don't want to be in your film." "If it was them." I pointed out the banana peel in an ashtray by the bed, coffee container from a café I frequented, a cheap carpenter's lamp clipped to a chair, a couple of books. "That was me," AC ambled away tipping painfully like he had a hip problem. I followed him into the big room. Someone Anna had once been charmed by.

"You see?" AC said. He pointed to places on the ceiling.

I didn't want to be here. Didn't need to be.

"That's where I had them installed, three of them." How much had he had on surveillance tape? An automated experimental documentary kind of unpredictable when it was all done had been his idea. "You needed burglars to make it work." "There wasn't much for them to take unless they really knew." Maybe he needed a narrative to thread this automated updated semi-silent, I ran my finger over some dust-greasy tomes of an encyclopedia.

AC found his cigarettes and his lighter. "1982 you danced on the beach. What happened to you?" "Us," I said.

"Was it when you were in California?" "Not only," I said, thinking how often I'd been to California. "These things are regrettable but sometimes I think they're going to happen anyway," AC said.

"Anyway?" I said. "It was me you wanted to kill," said AC. "It's too late now," I said. "Can't escape yourself fortunately."

"And your daughter. All grown up?" I had heard from her this morning. She was very good about that. AC shook his head. "Just goes to show."

I thought I would show my words when I got them all down in their rough state to Anna. Maybe not.

i spoke to her as a woman: she answered me as a man

an excerpt from *My Red Heaven*

Lance Olsen

hannah höch inadvertently completes kurt severing's thought

— *Berlin is a Dadaist photomontage*, she scribbles in the margins of her sketchbook, sitting on a crate in the storeroom at the back of a small gallery in Wedding, here from the Netherlands for a week to help set up her new show (the *vernissage* opening in half an hour), sleeping on a cot by night, by day helping repaint the walls, *all nonsense, travesty, incongruity, shock, noisy ephemeral machines that whir and clank but fail to function, instantaneous art that isn't pretty, proclaiming: Your belief in reason and progress did this, your bourgeois metaphysics, and we are here to end it.*

a brief history of the previous sentence

You were born thirty-eight years ago — not Hannah, but Anna: Anna Therese Johanne Höch — in Gotha, Thuringia, very near the precise geographic center of Germany, its pith, its crux, an area with almost nothing to recommend it, your parents removing you from school when you were fifteen to care for your youngest sister, but you sneaking back eight years later to study glass design and graphic arts in Berlin, your father having forbidden you to consider the various uselessnesses called painting and sculpture.

zurich café: version one

One evening in 1916 at the Cabaret Voltaire, Tristan Tzara picking up the French-German dictionary lying on the table next to his beer, opening it, and stabbing a random page with his letter opener.

The word the letter opener chooses is French babytalk for *hobbyhorse*.

In Rumanian it means *yes yes*.

In German, *get off my back*.

wish image : a.

I would like to show the world today as an ant sees it, Hannah scribbling in the storeroom, *and tomorrow as the moon sees it*, wondering about all the things she might mean by that — in the middle of it the door opening, the gallery owner popping in his head and saying:

It's time, Frau Höch. Shall we?

hand over woman's head

When I was six, I told my father I wanted to be an artist when I grow up. He looked down at me for a long moment and replied flatly: You can't do both, Anna.

a brief history of the previous sentence

In 1915 enrolling in a graphics class at the National Institute of the Museum of Arts and Crafts and falling in lust with Raoul Hausmann, that wide-mouthed, fat-egoed, monocle-wearing Austrian artist-writer-sound-poet and cofounder of the Berlin Dada circle.

Raoul's brain and cock, you coming to believe, were the transcendental incarnate.

Moving to the capital to be with him, landing a job in the handicrafts department for The Ullstein Press, designing dress and embroidery patterns for two of its magazines.

The Lady.

The Practical Berlin Woman.

three phrases from tzara's manifesto

1.   I am against manifestoes.
2.   Journalist virgins.
3.   *Boomboom, boomboom, boomboom.*

wish image : b.

Photomontage embodied our refusal to play the part of the artist, Hausmann explaining to an interviewer, already using the past tense. (It is 1927. It is an upscale restaurant off Savignyplatz, lunch courtesy of the interviewer's newspaper. The first automatic record changer has just been introduced, the first Volvo just premiered in Gothenburg, Bavaria just lifted its ban on Hitler's speeches, and Henry Ford just announced the production of the last Model T.) *We regarded ourselves as engineers, and our work as construction: we assembled our work, like a fitter.*

the practical berlin woman

We are delighted to report a new breed of female has appeared on our great city's streets. Let us call her The New Woman. She is smart and sophisticated, with an air of independence about her, and so casual about her looks, clothes, and manners as to be almost slapdash — in a wildly stylish fashion. She, we are certain, represents the wave of the future. We share her restlessness. We understand her determination to free herself from the shackles of the Great War's era and discover what life is really all about.

zurich café: version two

One evening in 1916 at the Cabaret Voltaire, Hugo Ball picking up the French-German dictionary lying on the table next to his beer, opening it, and stabbing a random page with his letter opener.

The word the letter opener chooses is French babytalk for *hobbyhorse.*

In Rumanian et cetera.

the painter
You having given anything to marry Raoul. All he had to do was agree to leave his wife. Your relationship with him would have thrived, you knew it, had he not regularly disparaged your desire to wed, calling it *your bourgeois inclination*. Had he not repeatedly proposed you might better spend your time sniffing out a better job to support him so he could get on with cleansing Germany's calcified society.

His behavior prompted you in 1920 to write the short story "The Painter," whose one-and-a-half-page narrative involves an artist who is thrown into an intense spiritual crisis when his wife asks him to do the dishes.

three phrases from hugo ball's manifesto
1.   Fog paroxysm.
2.   A cat meows.
3.   Dada m'dada dada mhm, dada dera dada, dada Hue, dada Tza.

hans richter reminisces about hannah höch's contribution to dada
Her input was extraordinarily beneficial to everyone — the way she could manage to conjure up sandwiches, beer, and coffee for us despite the shortage of money was remarkable.

zurich café: version three
One evening in 1916 at the et cetera, Richard Huelsenbeck et cetera.
Et cetera. Et —

wish image : c.
André Breton, one year before Hannah Höch steps into the crowded gallery on the arm of its owner: *Dada, very fortunately, is no longer an issue and its funeral, about May 1921, caused no rioting. Let there be Surrealism.*

wish image : d.
I thought the war would never end, George Grosz telling an interviewer in May 1959, two months before he drinks too much and jumbles down a

flight of stairs into death's arms. *And perhaps it never did.*

kurt schwitters reminisces about hannah höch's contribution to dada
We all live twenty-four minutes too late, don't we?

three phrases from richard huelsenbeck's manifesto
1.   A pig squeals in Butcher Nuttke's cellar.
2.   To sit in a chair for a single moment is to risk one's life.
3.

art history textbook, revised edition
It seems George Grosz and John Heartfield took against Höch's work almost immediately and aimed to have it excluded from the First International Dada Fair. Held between 30 June and 25 August 1920, the Berlin show subverted the traditional academic art exhibition by cramming the walls, ceiling, and floor of the small Galerie Otto Burchard on Lützowuferstraße with 174 posters, photomontages, and assemblages. Despite charging a considerable admission fee — three marks thirty, higher than the one cited in the catalogue — the enterprise proved a commercial failure. Höch was allowed to participate only when Hausmann threatened to withdraw his own work if hers was barred.

Most of what she exhibited there has been lost, but her large-scale photomontage, Cut with the Kitchen Knife Through the Last Weimar Beer-Belly Cultural Epoch in Germany — a forceful commentary on gender roles in the postwar years composed of a teeming array of texts and images spread across the canvas (Höch clipped and rearranged bits from product catalogues, printed broadsides, magazines, journals, and newspapers into her vast kaleidoscopic composition, then added watercolor highlights) — ironically turned out to be one of the most prominently displayed and well-received works of the show.

A photograph of Höch cradling one of her curious Dada dolls at the opening reveals her sporting an astonishing science-fiction get-up. That notwithstanding, she never relished the exhibitionist element of the movement. Rather, she was embarrassed by the bohemian antics of her male confederates — even if she often found herself appearing in supporting roles.

the manifesto hannah höch never wrote
Your belief in reason and progress did this, your bourgeois metaphysics, and we are here to end it.

My work on women's magazines woke me to the difference between media and reality. It provided me as well with the raw material for my project. I wanted to collect everything that seemed of value or might eventually be needed. I wanted to eat boundaries. I wanted to depict brides as the mannequins and machines and children they are.

The grammar of art, I discovered, is doubt.

i spoke to her as a woman, but she answered me as a man

Seven years after meeting Raoul Hausmann, you leaving him. Without a final conversation. Without a goodbye. You not being there anymore those last few months.

Although you are the one who brings about the split, the following year will prove the most depleted of your life. You looking inside yourself and finding only grief. Around your friends you pretending everything is all right. They pretending everything is all right back, believing that must be what you want.

It taking nearly four years to retrieve yourself from yourself. When you do, you discovering Mathilda Brugman walking by your side — Til, who likes to dress up as a man in a dark suit and tie, talk linguistics, and write poetry based sound, rhythm, and page design rather than meaning.

You moving to The Hague to be with her.

You moving back to Berlin together.

Your story a long happy ending until Til leaves you without a final conversation, without a goodbye. It hitting you after the fact that she hasn't been with you those last few months.

Your whole life, you coming to understand then, having been a science of imaginary solutions.

And so you marrying a traveling salesman twenty-two years younger than you, a convicted pedophile who likes to expose himself and jerk off in front of little girls in schoolyards, a man whom the German government will castrate not long before your wedding.

You marrying Kurt Matthies, aware before you your second date that you will divorce him within half a dozen years — although you never predicting Kurt will in fact leave you first for one of your closest girlfriends well before that.

wish image : e.

Fundamentally, André Breton telling an interviewer in July 1966, two months before he drifts off quietly among the readymades in his dreams, *since Dada we have done nothing.*

Doonesbury, Veal, and Titties

Ben Slotky

When Doonesbury creator Garry Trudeau was asked what he attributed his success to, his response was "Three words. Fat black titties."

I know.

I was as shocked as you are.

None of us were expecting to hear that, I don't think. I sure wasn't, I don't think.

Fat black titties?

That seems wrong on a lot of levels. The whole scenario does, actually. Why was I watching a press conference by the guy from Doonesbury? Why was this being televised?

I don't know, I have no idea. I almost choked on my veal when I heard it, but maybe not for the reasons you're thinking. I should explain this, I think. All or most of this.

I will back up.

I was at home pretending to watch a press conference from Garry Trudeau, the creator and cartoonist behind the Doonesbury comics. Doonesbury I think was a cartoon back in the 1980s. I am not sure I ever read it. When I first thought of this scenario, of me watching a televised press conference by the creator of Doonesbury, I thought maybe there was a character named Steve Dallas in it. There isn't. When I was a kid, I think I saw a Doonesbury cartoon called We're Eating More Beets! I eat a lot of beets now. I grind them up in a grinder. I put other things in there too. Kale, carrots, bananas. Blueberries and apples.

Honey. Flax seed. Peekaboo eggs.

I mix it all up and drink it.

Peanut butter.

Grind, grind. I mix up a lot of different things and make them into another thing, into a one thing. Then I drink that thing. I think I think that thing will make me healthy. I think I think that thing will make me feel better. Sometimes it does and sometimes it doesn't. Sometimes it do and sometimes it don't is a funny thing to say. I didn't used to do this, and by that I mean I didn't used to drink things that I'd turned into one thing. One time I ate veal, nothing but veal. This was a while ago. I was on an all-veal diet. High protein, high fear.

Low carb, high cruelty.

I wanted fear and cruelty and protein to be a large part of what I was ingesting. I wanted to subsume it, to consume it, to eat and eat it. There was a reason I was going to do this, I think, and not just because it was funny, even though doing something funny is a good reason to do something. Things that are funny are better than things that aren't funny, and you'd have to be a fat black titty not to know this.

I am the saddest man in the whole world. I am. You couldn't tell by looking at me, I don't think. I don't look sad, I don't think.

I look happy.

I am always smiling. I am smiling right now, now as I read this. I may have been smiling when I wrote this, I don't know. I don't remember. I bet I was, though. I bet I was. Now as I read this, there are some of you laughing. I am looking at you now. Looking at you and smiling. I am not sure what you are laughing at. It could be any number of things, I guess.

Maybe you are laughing about the things I said about Doonesbury. There were some funny things in there. The whole premise was funny, really. What a way to start a story! And that title? Hilarious. That is funny. Maybe you are laughing about that. That could be. Maybe you are laughing about the veal. It's funny, that part is.

Talking about veal is funny. What we talk about when we talk about talking about veal; that's what this part of the story would be called if people called parts of stories things. Maybe that is a thing people will do in the future, talk about parts of stories rather than whole stories. Maybe it will be like that. That would be funny if it was, I think. Maybe you're laughing about me saying I am the saddest man in the world. That doesn't seem funny to me at all. I'm wondering why you would laugh at that. I'm wondering what kind of person would laugh at that, at a person being the saddest person in the world. I am envisioning somebody laughing right now, laughing at the words I'm saying, the words I've written. Maybe they are laughing at the arrangement of words. Maybe they are laughing at the idea of words themselves. The notion of words.

Words and letters.

So ridiculous.

Symbols, characters, letters, words.

Arranged and arranged.

Put together, fit and pieced.

Doonesbury and titties and veal.

For effect, for impact.

Peanut butter and seeds.

Designed.

That's funny, I think. That whole thing is, and it's getting to be not funny. Not funny all of a sudden, and it's like this, and it's like this all the time, all the time, and maybe that is why I'm so sad. Maybe I'm sad because things that are funny become not funny. Maybe I'm sad because there are things. Maybe I'm sad because I know I have to keep arranging things, things and words, words and letters, until I am not sad anymore. Maybe I'm sad because someday I will run out of beets and Doonesburys. Of veal and fat black titties

from *The Grey Area*

Ken Edwards

The tide was in at Deadmans Beach, and the wind was up. The
fishing fleet was ranged on the banks of shingle being encroached
by rushing and receding waves: an impressive if heterogeneous
collection of chiefly traditionally clinker-built vessels (but some
of fibreglass), both larger trawlers and also punts, that's to say,
undecked boats, all with diesel engines, sitting on their greased
hardwood blocks or planks, awaiting favourable conditions. Linseed
oil dully gleamed and colours faded against the whitening sky.
Winch engines and their cables, some apparently half consumed by
corrosion, also lay dormant, and among them the detritus of a fishing
beach: walls and labyrinths of creels, plastic and wooden boxes or
their fragments, piles of greasy nets. Two or three men wandered
between the huts; one called briefly to another – but this was all the
human life that could be observed. A crushed, stained white latex
glove and a dirty, crumpled T-shirt with the Superman logo that had
evidently been employed as a rag lay discarded on the intervening
gravel. Used plastic bottles were scattered here and there. On the
casing of a winch, a hand-painted notice in white lettering on a black
ground: KEEP OFF. On the shingle banks, eviscerated fish corpses
and emptied skulls stank and were disdained by the ragged flocks of

gulls, terns and plovers that edged the moving foam. From the sterns of various boats fluttered black flags on tall poles. Some vessels had names painted on their bows or sterns, for example: *Moonshine, Candice Marie, Zelda, The Brothers Grim, David Bowie, Blackbeard, Our Dot & Danny, Little Mayflower, King Hell, Safe Return.* Their registration numbers were prominently displayed in most cases, and the following were noted: DB11, DB16 (etc, all the way up to...) DB590 – DB signifying that the boats were registered in the port of Deadmans Beach. All in all, including small row boats and others whose registration numbers were obscured or not present, a total of twenty-eight vessels were counted.

A huge volume of water appeared to be driven repeatedly and relentlessly by the strong breeze – verging on gale – onto the beach. The line of undulations could be tracked like a moving graph against the concrete groyne that marked the south-western boundary of the fishing beach, in the lee of which was suddenly observed a shining black creature – at first glance a seal, but quickly revealed to be a solitary surfer in black wetsuit, crouching, waiting for the right wave to arrive. And so this mysterious being watched the approach of a tall one with rippling white foam at its rim; the foam starting to glitter, for the sun only then began to make its presence felt through the white banks of cloud, the shoreward wall of the wave now being in shadow, and darkening further as it rose.

But the wave seemed to pause. And at the last possible moment the surfer took advantage, and, embracing his electric blue board tightly as one would a newly refound lover, launched himself into the van of the approaching current that swept him inexorably shoreward, showing only a flash of his orange flippers, before it broke over him in a white explosion. Then just as the figure seemed lost, he reappeared in the midst of the retreating water, struck out and began to swim back where he'd come from, following the flowback to the lee of the groyne, where he would turn, shelter and repeat the experience.

The fishing community's favourite hostelry, enquiries quickly established, was the Richard the Lionheart Inn.

Set back from the front and faced by the fishermen's tar-black wooden sheds that flank the shingle beach, it presented as an ancient inn that had seen better days and had somehow survived misjudged attempts at modernisation on the cheap: a tiled roof, tall chimneys, with weatherboarding at the front and hanging tiles on the sides filling the spaces between modern UPVC windows. Vertical rust-streaks down the wall bearded the cast iron brackets for hanging baskets that bore no blooms at this time of year. Pasted inside the front windows were posters for local bands: Monday nights were blues nights, Saturday nights featured a wider variety of genres, including a psychedelic option. Entry to the bar was via a short flight of stone steps flanked by railings.

Fluttering on high: the red-on-white cross, emblem of the Crusaders.

The south-westerly was beginning to pump up seriously now, and with it came flecks of rain, so entering the pub was a welcome relief, the more so as ale from a respected regional brewery was advertised. The interior was badly lit. The only other customers, seated on high stools at opposite ends of the long bar, were an elderly man with hair in long white ringlets descending to his shoulders, wearing a black jacket, khaki cargo pants and impeccably white trainers, slowly supping a pint; and an overweight woman, who was engaged in shouting at the barman. She too wore white trainers, but quite scuffed, and black trousers, and her anorak was open to reveal a pink poodle on her sweater. She cradled a glass of something with lemon in it.

The low ceiling, crisscrossed by beams, featured giant crabs and other marine creatures trapped there by netting; paddles, flags and lifebelts decorated the walls, also a dartboard, and a noticeboard pinned with photographs and advertisements for forthcoming events. At the far end, next to the toilets, a much scrubbed blackboard advertised the dishes *du jour.* These included soup, the idea of which appealed.

So what, then, was the soup of the day?

Vegetable.

A deal was struck with the young, monosyllabic barman: soup and a pint, a table in the corner claimed.

Giles, cried the lady in the poodle sweater, addressing the ringleted elder from her end of the bar.

Closer observation now revealed that this snowy-haired gentleman was wearing makeup and eyeliner, and his fingernails were polished in a fetching shade of teal. What's that, my dear? he said.

Have you finished planning your funeral?

As a matter of fact, yes, Dodie, if you really want to know.

You going for burial at sea?

(Giles turned to our corner to acknowledge the presence of the outside world in this enclave.)

Highly irregular, of course. (Palm vertical on the side of his mouth, he continued in a stage whisper with a wink for our benefit:) Mum's the word.

So you going to be dumped over the side, then?

Dodie, there will be more to it than that. You make me sound like an illegal catch.

I always thought you were! And Dodie, spectacles glinting, laughed uproariously at her own witticism.

The padre has agreed to be involved, just between us, you understand. There'll be a ceremony, of sorts. Prayers will be said. I *am* a man of faith, you know.

I knew you were, Giles, said Dodie, you believe in God, don't ya.

I prefer to speak about the Author of everything in this world, both seen and unseen.

But you believe in Him.

I don't know so much about that, but I trust that *He* believes in *us*. You understand what I'm saying?

You're a one, Giles.

If the Author doesn't believe in us, who else is going to?

I dunno.

The Author of all things knows where we're going.

And He believes in us?

It could be a She, conceded Giles.

Maybe He or She hasn't got a clue, was the poodle lady's suggestion.

Well, you've got to trust they do. It's trust more than belief, you know what I mean? That's what you call faith.

And you think you're going to Heaven?

We are, said Giles solemnly, already living in Paradise.

Could've fooled me, said the poodle lady.

Deadmans Beach. Every morning when the light comes

up here in Deadmans Beach I give thanks for another day that's
been given me. It is fucking Paradise, is it not, excuse my language,
mister.

(He received an assurance from our quarter that no offence
was taken at bad language.)

Yeah, it is nice here, admitted Dodie. I wouldn't live nowhere
else now.

We all drank.

Are you down from London, then? inquired Giles of us.

In a manner of speaking. And you?

Born and bred in Deadmans Beach, myself. Proud of it.
She's from London, she's a bloody DFL, he added, pointing with his
pint mug at Dodie, who burst into another loud cackle of laughter.

I've only been here thirty years, Giles!

You've served your apprenticeship then.

I'll say. And don't call me *she*. You're a very rude man, Giles,
I don't care if God believes in you or not, it's a fact. Me old man it
was (Dodie went on for our benefit), who brought me here when we
got married. He was in the fishing trade all his life. But he passed on,
what is it, two year ago.

We expressed our sorrow at her loss, and there was a brief
silence to mark it.

You down on business then, or holiday-making or what?
continued Giles politely.

Our assurance that there was no holiday-making involved
met with general approval.

A private investigator? Blimey, that's something new, ain't it,
Dodie? We haven't had one of them down here before. But you're not
with the police then?

By no means. And your secret is safe.

Secret?

The burial at sea.

It was Giles' turn to laugh, which he did quite lustily.

Of course, scattering ashes at sea is perfectly legal, we
pointed out. But an intact, unburnt body, that's quite a different
matter.

You are correct, sir, it is against the law, but it happens all
the time in the fishing community, explained Giles. Quite regularly
you get a church funeral, somebody local, and the bearers may

notice the casket is unusually light. You follow my drift? Everybody knows what that means.

The body is not there?

Exactly. The real funeral occurs under cover of darkness. Boat pulls out to sea as per usual a day or so later, when the tide and weather conditions are right – maybe more than one boat, depends on how many mourners, you see. Out a couple of miles, then … well, I don't need to spell it out.

Understood.

It's important to us. Well, I was in the fishing for many years. Can't say I chose it, but I was brought up to it, like. It's a hard life, but it's still in my blood, even though I've been retired for longer than I care to remember. And so I want to go back to the bosom of the sea when my time comes.

It seemed an apt moment to bring up, discreetly, the subject of our investigation.

Edith Watkins? Giles frowned into his drink.

I remember her, volunteered Dodie. Lady what disappeared.

She wasn't the one who – ?

She used to go for her walks along here, Giles, you remember, she talked to everybody? Edie, that's what we called her. Little Edie.

Did she come into the pub?

Not often. I seen her in here with a cup of coffee sometimes. Maybe once or twice. I don't think she drank.

She wasn't the one who wangled herself a trip on a fishing boat, was that the one, Dodie?

That is the one, Giles, that was, what, ten or twenty year ago, she was a brave lady. Getting on even then, a bit mad, you know, but anyway she disappeared last year, it was on the news. Come on, you must remember?

Yes, I recall Little Edie now. Haven't seen her for … ooh, donkey's years. So is she dead?

The police, we explained, had not been able to determine this, and looked unlikely to, but it seemed that her last journey might have involved a visit to the waterfront.

So what do you think, she might have stowed away on a boat and fallen off the side? exclaimed Dodie with great excitement.

It was necessary to reassure the pair that this was not a

leading theory, and that the task at hand was simply to establish
her movements on the last day she had been seen alive. Neither,
however, could recall when precisely they had last seen her. Nor
could they remember any police inquiries last year, and the name of
DCI Green meant nothing to them.

Who was it, Giles demanded of Dodie, who took her out on
that fishing trip a few years ago, was it old Gallop, you know, Doc
Gallop? I have a feeling now it was.

Yes, that's right, old Doc, bless him.

Would it be possible to speak to Mr Gallop? was our inquiry.

You'd have a job, said Giles.

Why so?

He died.

Buried at sea?

Who knows? Don't ask, don't tell.

But his son still runs the same boat, said Dodie, he'll have
known her better than us. Darren Gallop, he's the president of the
Fishermen's Association now.

So he should be easy to contact?

Comes in here a lot, said Giles. Partial to a pint in the old
Dick, is the younger Gallop. Very eminent man these days, though.
The *Jumpy Mary*, that's his boat. You'll find him in the book, or just
call in here again. He'll be around anyway, nobody's going out fishing
in this weather.

And as he drained his pint mug the fingernails flashed briefly
like blue jewels.

How was your soup, sir? was everything all right? asked the
quiet young barman, who had suddenly appeared on this side of the
counter with a wiping cloth.

He was reassured as to the quality of both the fare and the
service.

Dodie stood down from the bar, zipped up her anorak,
concealing the pink poodle from view.

Where you going now, my love? asked Giles.

Never you mind. Nice meeting you, mister.

And you.

I am going out for A Fag – *should* anyone inquire.

Ooh, lovely, my dear, I'm sure.

I didn't mean you, Giles. See ya.

Filthy habit, commented Giles when she'd gone. As filthy as the weather.

He motioned to the barman for another pint. We attempted to pay for this, but he would not hear of it.

from *Growing Dumb*
Chapter Eight. Teachers and Pupils

Peter Quartermain

In Prep School we simply couldn't get away from Mrs Bailey locking
us down with her watchful eye, she didn't smile much and she hardly
ever laughed, and she made sure we never got up to mischief.
"You're not in here to enjoy yourselves," she said again and again,
"You're here to learn" and as soon as Break started she shooed us
all outside. *You can't be in here when I'm not. Go and play.* We spent
a lot of the time doing what I'd done in Wheaton Aston, endless drills
in the times-tables, lots of practice at copperplate handwriting in our
Rough Books and in our copying books once she'd found some,
. (. (. (. (. (a a a a a printed along one line, a blank line
underneath so you could copy, then *ℬ ℬ ℬ ℬ ℬ b b b b b* on the
next, dip your pen in the ink, stay carefully between the lines and
draw the loopy Victorian letters, whatever you do don't muddle up
the thick strokes and the thin strokes. And when you've finished
this page go on to the next, by the end of the book you're joining
the letters into words, real writing. It was just like what I'd done at
Rushbury or even two years ago at Woodroughs in Shirley, and just
like then it was too easy to muddle the thick and the thin, when I put
my pen down and then picked it up again or shifted my grip after
wiping the nib clean, nobody'd ever bothered to show me or anyone

else how to hold the pen at its proper slope, or said a word about the nib and at what sort of angle, we all watched each other to see, but woe betide if you made a mess in your copying book.

Mrs Bailey taught Dictation, Composition, and Literature, that's what English was, but mostly we did handwriting and dictation. When we did Literature we read things out loud, simplified stories out of Macaulay and Lamb's *Tales from Shakespeare*, Horatio at the Bridge or a prosy version of *Twelfth Night*, Mrs Bailey said Malvolio was funny in his yellow stockings but she didn't explain, I couldn't understand it at all *Why was it alright for them all to laugh at him like that? He hadn't done anything wrong.* It just didn't make sense, all these people being so cruel *Whoever'd want to be laughed at?* It wasn't fair. Yet when we read about Mucius Scaevola driving Lars Porsena away from the gates of Rome by sticking his hand in the fire without even a quail, he was so heroic, and I thought of me having my tonsils out proud that I'd been sick seven times. I might have read that story in History, sometimes we got Mr Pearce instead of Mrs Bailey, but we certainly weren't taught anything about how the Romans destroyed and obliterated Etruscan language and culture. People talked a lot of the time even in School about how the Germans were trying to obliterate us, and like a lot of the songs we had in Music, everything, all the stories, were about Heroes, Hector and Lysander, Drake, Raleigh and Nelson, poems by Sir Henry Newbolt and Alfred Noyes. Learn "Drake's Drum" by heart, and Charles Wolfe's 1817 poem "The Burial of Sir John Moore at Corunna," I've never read that again, not since, but over seventy years later I can still remember bits, even though I didn't quite understand what was going on:

> Not a drum was heard, not a funeral note,
> As his corse to the rampart we hurried;
> Not a soldier discharged his farewell shot
> O'er the grave where our hero we buried.

Mrs Bailey taught us Arithmetic too, addition subtraction multiplication and division as well as pounds shillings and pence, she'd write sums on the board and then we'd do them, sometimes on the board, more often in our Rough Books, and we learned about columns for tens and units and how to do long division and we learned about fractions. One night I lay awake in the dormitory for ages smiling to myself but puzzled at the name Vulgar Fractions and wondered what Marlow Grandmother thought about *them*, were they somehow bad, like Urchins, and not at all like Proper Nouns? I didn't dare ask; Mrs Bailey didn't invite questions.

Nevertheless Prep School was alright, I even almost liked it quite a bit of the time, we were all in it together, we had no classes on Wednesday and Saturday afternoons, there wasn't a lot of homework, we called that *Prep*, and we could get outside where the teachers weren't watching us all the time not even when we were supposed to be watching a School Team at soccer or cricket, and we had a lot of different things to do each day during the week. Once or sometimes twice a week we'd troop over to the Lower Pitch for a double period of Games. But once Summer Term came along we didn't go there at all it was so gloomy. And we didn't play cricket, not in Games. For Games, on a hot day we marched in a crocodile down to the disused Swimming Pool at the bottom of Bath Field, there wasn't much water, just a stream running through silt and mud at the bottom of the big square-walled empty pool, willow herb and plantain enjoying the sun and moisture, we stayed clear of a bed of nettles near the shallow end steps. Mrs Bailey'd watch us from her perch on her shooting-stick as we went down into the empty pool the stream running in a trough it'd carved in the sand and mud through the middle before it left under the sluice gate at the deep end, she'd just sit and watch, making sure we didn't stray out of sight, weeds and thistles and grass and stuff growing in the mud and silt piled up by the stream over the winter, sometimes a cow had got in there and left a great cowpat, if it was close to the stream one or two of us'd try to ease it in so it'd wash away it might even float, we'd scrape little paths in the sandbanks and the mud for the water to flow and we'd build dams and play pooh-sticks and just soss about wading, of course someone'd slip in the mud and fall full length in the stream, sometimes land on a stone on the sandbank and before long everybody'd be chucking water about, once or twice a couple of kids had old seaside pails they'd remembered to bring, or if we could get away with it fill a paper bag with water to make a bomb, but *No!*, Mrs Bailey'd say, *You mustn't waste paper!* and it wasn't till after the War that we learned to drop water-bombs from the dorm windows onto daykids or any other deserving victim but not on another boarder if you could help it, mud'd fly everywhere, bits of cowpat with it, noisy horseplay lots of shouting, all of us soaked. Mrs Bailey'd just sit there on her shooting stick in her tweeds and cloche hat. She never got wet.

The water was quite deep, a couple of feet anyway, where it went through the sluice-gate, it hadn't been closed for years but the stream rushed through there on its way to the culvert under the canal, if we got at all close she'd call us back, and after a couple of trips to the pool some of us discovered that with innocence or absentmindedness all over your face you could with a shifty sort of sleight of body sneak out of sight at the shallow end upstream where she didn't look, the water quiet and shallow as it flowed through the entrance to the pool, she kept her eye on the depth at the sluice-gate, the current, I'd quietly wade upstream through the gap in the walls, the stream banks quite sharp just there and once past the wall she couldn't see me, what a pleasure that was, to be out of her sight, in the shade under the hawthorns hanging over the stream, soft muddy bottom dead twigs all waterlogged caught in it perhaps a few thorns here and there tread carefully but nothing much, dappled light, behind me a trail of muddy smudges in the water from where my feet'd been, just the slow sound of the stream, it only sped up at the sluice gate, branches a faint shush I could hardly hear as they trailed along the water, I really had to listen hard, their faint background noise almost hidden by the steady in-and-out of my breath my heart-beat getting in the way, slight gurgle of water round my legs, the sounds of the other kids talking and laughing and splashing back in a bright sunlit world, goosebumps at the sudden chill of shadowed breeze. I quietly splashed up the stream, little eddies with long-legged boatmen scooting across the surface, midges and gnats maybe a dragonfly or two, tiddlers and even sticklebacks here and there as well as tadpoles or frogs, perhaps a bird's nest but you had to know where to look, minnows by the hundreds scooting off at my cautious step or at my shadow, there might even be a cow on the bank having a drink, deep muddy hoofprints at the water's edge crushing tufts of grass and filling with water, mixed cool smells, rabbit droppings, a thrush or blackbird calling, or the wonderful chittering mellow song of a robin, so tuneful some kids we scoffed at thought it was really a nightingale *As if a nightingale would sing in the daytime!*, and if you got missed then a shout, your name faint on the air. If you'd got any sense you went back down the stream, you could say you were just round the corner not really out of sight, but not if you came back along the grass you'd be in for it *Where have you been? How dare you go up there!* But she was less forbidding even then, there wasn't any danger and she knew it, but there I was one time looking to left and right at the jungle undergrowth my pistol a forked twig in my right hand just above my waist *Got to keep it dry* looking out for the German spies in their pith helmets and rifles, there were two of them the fat one who slobbered and drooled a lot and the thin brutal one with a monocle *Achtung! Wir da?* with a curl of his lip cold and contemptuous, I'd better make sure their Overseers didn't see me with their huge bull-whips, could I get through and rescue Algy and Ginger *How did they get into such a mess this time?* can't wait till dark got to get back to camp by then *Must check Dusky's alright, that's a nasty wound in his leg* and as I silently crept up the Orinoco the ground gave way beneath me *Quicksand!* I floundered back waving my arms dropped my stick huge *Splash!* I went right under, *uuuurgh* my hair all wet Mrs Bailey'd be cross we weren't supposed to get our hair wet, I turned back my heart pounding away *I bet it really was quicksand* my foot hadn't touched bottom just really soft soft mud just like water really but squishy *There was no footing at all!* I'd lurched my weight onto my back foot *Horrible way to die* grabbed at a branch over my head *sluggish heavy bubbles bursting through thick ooze pith helmet sitting on smooth mud slow ripple as a finger broke the surface then subsided into the glop a desperate heave then everything flat and still* good job I'd missed, it was hawthorn, that'd've hurt, and when I got back to the Swimming Pool all in a rush I was still a bit panicky somebody said "Did you go very far up the stream then? Herrick said there's lots of potholes up there, they're not deep but they'll give you a start if you tread in one, pebbles and stuff in the bottom, nothing nasty," and I grinned, a bit quavery, but I didn't say anything.

Nor did Mrs Bailey, sitting there in the warm sun. The deep lines round her mouth softened a bit, her gaze drifted as she let go a bit, she wasn't watching very hard, us out of her clutches mucking about in mud and water too happy to be squabbling, her settled on her shooting stick or even down on the dry and sunny grass, us larking about, none of us bothered by all the mud in our hair or on our trunks and shouting as much as we wanted down in the baths. But after a while I began to shiver a bit whenever a cloud hid the sun, I didn't want to go back to the water to wash the mud off, but when I looked at a couple of the others, standing in the shadow made by the pavilion I saw a muscle on Arnold's thigh jump a bit and suddenly I couldn't stop shivering and I wanted my tea, wanted the shivery walk to School to clean up properly, wet muddy towels damp hair hardly any of us with energy enough to run about, we didn't even have to march in crocodile and we were allowed to talk.

We had English and Arithmetic every day with her, and some days, in between we had History and Geography but she didn't teach them much, we mostly got Mr Pearce for those and Miss Ogden for French, but because of the War they had to do a lot of the teaching in the real School, so we didn't see them very much, and soon we mostly got away from her twice a week when we had Music and Drawing, we didn't do them in Rushall but in different rooms. I used to love Drawing, it's odd I don't remember anything at all about it except the pleasure it felt so very different from everything else we did, I have no idea who taught it before the beginning of 1944 when Angus Beaton came, I know we had Art classes, there's marks in my Report Book, in my first Term I got 40% so I don't suppose I was any good, don't think I learned anything but then I don't think anybody actually taught anything till Angus came, probably couldn't draw really just looked after us for forty minutes with pencil and paper, or perhaps you had your own paintbox, classes were in a square wooden building, one of the new classrooms jutting out into the Croft back of the School, it'd been specially designed for teaching Art. A lot of the Teachers in the School were like Walrus Wroth too old to be in the Army or had been wounded, the War ran through a lot of Teachers and the School had to make do with whoever it could get. Sometimes when we came back to School at the beginning of Term we had new Teachers who were only there for one Term and sometimes when we came back there wasn't a Teacher at all in some subjects. When Phil went there in January 1940 "woodwork" was taught by Mrs Bailey's father, a retired carpenter who'd come to help out and really loved the splendidly-equipped carpentry workshop, he know how to use it all, but he'd gone when I got there eighteen months later. By then there was nobody to teach Greek or Latin, anyone who knew French or German was away as an interpreter no matter how old they were.

When I went home for the summer in 1943 we'd been living in Rugby for a year, by then I was just over nine and I'd begun to take Science, but there hadn't been any Geography or French that Term and when I came back in September all there was was English and Arithmetic and Games, there wasn't even a report on the Music or Drawing I'd been taking forever and my Report Book looked very incomplete. History and Geography and Science and French had disappeared except in the upper forms and Mr Bailey wasn't there any more at all by Christmas, there was just a rubber-stamp instead of his signature and no comments at all where the Headmaster's Report was supposed to be. Henry Houston was the Acting Headmaster all that Term, he signed Our Kid's Report Book and wrote "conduct &c – excellent," that's all he said, but I don't think any of that bothered me very much even though Mrs Bailey was still there, and Mum and Dad nearly withdrew us from Brewood altogether, there was a chance the School might close anyway.

Mrs Bailey was always there, of course, she was the Headmaster's Wife, and it was her who ran the Prep School. Report Book or no the Music Teacher was always there too, Moggie Morris, till 1946 at any rate when I was in the Fourth Form, he'd been called out of retirement, later on we had Walrus to teach us math and he'd been retired too, white hair and raggy moustache, stoop-shouldered, and like Moggie Morris he was a terrible teacher, just stood up there and told us things, didn't talk to us at all but shouted a lot and looked bad-tempered. Moggie was simply hopeless, we endured him and his silvery long hair and his frayed grey chalk-stripe suit and his badly-polished shoes. We had Music classes in Big School, twenty or twenty-five kids sitting on wooden PT benches up close against the stage, him sitting at the piano up there on the stage, one day a week there'd be a blackboard and easel, the other day just the piano, when he'd hand out song books and he'd play and we'd sing, "The Lincolnshire Poacher" was a favourite, lively thumping good tune

Oh it's my delight of a Friday night

In the season of the year

or even better a song I've never heard since then but Our Kid still knows the words more than sixty years later, as do I, and we can both sing it with as great gusto now as we did then, carolling and chirping away at each other over the telephone

There was an old man named Michael Finnegan

He grew whiskers on his chinnegan

> The wind came out and blew them innegan
> Poor old Michael Finnegan!

We just loved the recital of his adventures and his downfalls, he climbed a tree and barked his shinnegan, and we really enjoyed those classes, exercising our lungs as the songs echoed and boomed round the big empty room along with the endless parade of military and patriotic songs sung with a lot of swozz. We sang *The British Grenadiers* so much that I still shudder over the inexorable "Hector and Lysander and such great men as these," I cannot drive them from my mind, but Moggie's great love was for genteel Victorian parlour songs and folksongs, the sentimentality of *Danny Boy* sung to the Londonderry Air, and of *Annie Laurie*'s "Maxwelton braes are bonnie," which he played again and again insisting we hold the notes properly and sing the songs "beautifully" because we'd be singing them on stage in front of our parents and visitors from the village when the School Concert came round. Rehearse and rehearse and rehearse again, "No No NO! You all start on the count of *four*! and you, Jones, you're terrible, is your voice breaking, at *your* age? you're no good, keep absolutely quiet until the second line!" Syncopation was completely alien to him, he despised it, I think I was an undergraduate at Nottingham and had joined the jazz club before I even heard the word. Once at the end of Term it must have been about 1945 when I was just over eleven and the average age of the Form was twelve-and-a-half, when he said he'd play us anything we wanted as a special treat, Music that year wasn't in Big School but in the Art Room, one of the older kids it might have been Bogey Butcher he was really big dark hair slicked back he had a lot of muscle he was just beginning to grow hair on his face he must have been nearly fourteen and had spots, said from the back of the room "Play 'Home Sweet Home Again' Sir," you could hear the smirk in his voice and his spotty-faced pals laughed, it was a pop song on the wireless, Joe Loss and His Band, I didn't like it very much but it was the sort of song that stuck in your head whether you wanted it to or not, an ear-worm, we all knew the words, and Moggie shifted gravely on the piano bench and said "Good, you're beginning to learn something after all; you want 'Home Sweet Home' again" and launched forth:

> Mid pleasures and palaces
> Though we may roam,

> Be it never so humble,
>
> There's no-o place like home!

we'd heard him play it and'd had to sing it beautifully too many times
all year, and we hated it almost as much as we hated "Come Into
the Garden Maud" except *that* made us laugh it was so silly, and I
wanted to pipe up "Please Sir that's the wrong song, he wanted the
one that goes like this," but I knew my face'd be red and my voice
a strangled squeak, I wanted to sing it to him to show the big boys
in the room that I understood even if Mr Morris did not, I didn't want
them to look down on me, they walked about owning the place, I
wanted to be on their side I wanted them in their unruliness to be
on my side, but I was, blessedly, too timid to interrupt him once he'd
started playing the song and singing it to us, everybody in the room
would've laughed at me he'd probably have walloped me if I'd said it.
I started to say it but shut up and nobody noticed. I was frightened
by Mr Morris, and they were not. And I saw more of him than they
did.

Once a week I had piano lessons from him. I'd go down to the Dining
Hall in a free period or at the end of classes, the big room empty
except for the mild clatter from the kitchen as Cook and Miss Butler
got tea ready for all the boarders or lunch for the whole School,
the tables all set up with plates and cutlery, cups and saucers, him
waiting as I came in through the big double doors all us boys had to
use, the whole length of the room between me with my music and
him with a handful of music, sometimes an exercise he'd written out
for me on music paper, my boots echoed round the room and he'd
nod and say "Sit down." Just him and me. No other kids. I couldn't
think of him as Moggie, he was Mr. Morris. Nothing to divert his
attention. The back of my leg shied from the cold wood of the piano
bench, him at my right elbow on a padded chair he'd taken from
High Table just behind us where the Headmaster and the Masters
ate their meals, faint goose-flesh at the small scratch of his suit
against my arm as he reached across to the music. He always
made me adjust the bench, I never got it where he wanted it to be,
"You're too far back," he'd say, or "you've got it crooked," and when I
finished pushing and pulling and shuffling about a bit, my feet hardly

reached the pedals never mind the floor he'd say "Now, play me your scales." I never did get the fingering right, except for C, I'd get terribly confused in A or D and especially in E, and he'd get very cross very quickly, he had a wooden rod or sometimes a ruler which he'd use as a baton and he'd beat hard on the misbehaving fingers, *snap!* It hurt, "NO! Why don't you listen? D *sharp* in E, can't you *hear* it?" and he'd finger through it quickly "Like *this!* Use the *correct* fingering" or he'd bang me across the wrist, "Hold the hand like this, boy!" and he'd lean back and sigh, and I'd blink back tears, you should *never* cry in front of a Master. And try again. "Practice, boy, practice! Why don't you practice? An hour every day!" but of course I always had an exciting book to read or someone had got a game of Polly-on-the-Mop or Releasio going in Big School or the weather was much too nice to be stuck indoors, the Dining Hall was a cold and lonely place to be struggling at the piano, the kitchen maids would come in about some task or other and give me a quick glance but I didn't dare notice, it'd be too furtive and he'd see. Or on other days I'd be sitting in a cold island of light, the rest of the room dark, the windows blacked out and it getting close to bedtime. By the end of every lesson my hands would be red and feel raw and I simply hated it but Mum and Dad were paying extra for the lessons and Our Kid was taking them too and *he* could play, he actually liked practicing, much later when he'd got his own business he even bought a grand piano. But quite often I'd go to Matron on days I had Piano and tell her I felt sick I'd miss breakfast and she'd keep me in bed all day, she must have known I was lying she must have noticed I was always sick on the same day malingering away but I got away with it, when I went back to Moggie after missing two classes he'd be a bit more friendly and ask me if I felt better and let me get away with mistakes without losing his temper.

I didn't think it then but of course he'd spent all day listening to reluctant small boys who like me hadn't practiced much all week botching their scales and their exercises. He endured us as much as we endured him, more. As I look back I realise he was always more even-tempered early in the day, but the music and the exercises were so boring, you just played plod plod plod, there were never any tunes and everything was in two-four time, bink-bonk bink-bonk, he never but once gave me a lively tune to learn and that time I did practice, at the next lesson I played it right through and I surprised

him and me both, I enjoyed it, it was something he'd written, "by
T. Granville Morris" it said on the cover, published by Boosey &
Hawkes, or perhaps it was Novello but I don't think so, he was proud
of it, but even in the lesson where I started out playing his piece
properly right through I made mistakes later on and he used his ruler,
I was still afraid of him and his temper.

Once a week in Music class he'd teach Music Theory, there'd
be a blackboard and easel on the Gym stage, we all had half-size
notebooks, the right-hand page ruled like music-manuscript and the
left just like a regular notebook and he'd tell us about music, how
important "Grand Opera" was, the big room so empty and echoey we
all heard "Ground Opera," and wondered what it was, "Is it because
they stand on the dirt, Sir?" "NO, Boy!" he'd shout, "Pay attention!
Don't be so rude!" or "Use the brains God gave you, Child!" Perhaps
he'd scrawl it on the board but his handwriting was so bad and the
board so pockmarked and battered you couldn't tell if he'd written an
a or an *o*, he'd talk about great arias and he'd talk about composers
whose names we'd dutifully write down, like Vargner and Showpan,
some of the kids knew how to spell them but most of us didn't and
we never handed our books in mine was all blots and smudges,
but the bigger kids, the ones that knew what the names really were
would bait him, all the years he taught at Brewood, they ragged him
all the time because the classes were so dull, and unlike us small
kids they got away with it. I didn't know where to look, couldn't rest
my eyes anywhere but felt a bit cold and sweaty and cringed when
they really got going, worrying that Moggie'd notice me. Or that *they*
would. "When they sing, Sir, is it like the Walsall 'Arriers, Sir?" that
was the name of a well-known local running club, and somebody
else would chime in with a suppressed laugh "Do they run about
while they sing their arias, Sir?" They had no fear of him at all, and
certainly no respect, he didn't know at all how to deal with more than
one child at a time and was unsure even then, he was useless as a
disciplinarian, and to those of us who didn't take Private Lessons he
was a figure of fun, the way Angus Beaton would be later on when
he came to the School to teach Art and suffered just as much from
the rotten beaten-up blackboards and bad handwriting as Moggie
Morris had.

In History of Art we'd get to class to find the blackboard
covered with a set of notes we had to copy into our notebooks,

Angus'd be standing there his greenish checked-tweed suit all dusty with chalk a propelling pencil clipped into his top pocket, he never wore a gown, like Moggie Morris he didn't have one, the board all white speckles from kids chucking things about the room over the years. There was no such thing as blackboard paint, not in the War. As soon as we'd all got the left-hand board copied he'd rub it out and fill it up again with new stuff while we copied the right, his suit looking baggier and baggier as he scrunched over to reach the bottom of the board, "Please, Sir," somebody would say, we loved to vex him, "it says on the board 'Corot was born in Paris in 1796 at the age of 26.' 'Ow did 'e manage that, Sir?" and Angus would raise an eyebrow go a bit pink look at the board and as he turned to make the comma after "1796" bigger so we could see it, somebody else would say "Was he born in 1770, Sir?" and he'd look a bit blank. "Is that a full stop after 'Paris,' Sir? Did he start painting in 1796?" and we'd all laugh a bit. He had a wonderful pixyish sort of elfin face, hooked eyebrows, not much hair, and he'd look a bit cross but he'd shrug as he gazed at that poxed blackboard and gesture vaguely, his slightly pointed ears stirring as he swallowed, "You know what it says," he'd say, and you could tell he was suppressing a tiny quirk of a grin at the same time as he was exasperated, he found us a bit tiresome and he endured us, we knew enough to drop it, not go too far, we liked him too well for that, he was impatiently good-humoured, he was too courteous to say "Shut up, Jones, and don't be impertinent," too gentle, and in Drawing class he'd pay close attention to how you were doing, he attracted us in ways Moggie Morris didn't, he'd lean over your shoulder and sketch a line in, his asthmatic wheeze in your ear he'd been gassed in the First World War he'd been in the trenches like Dad I suppose but I never really made the connection for ages and ages, we had no idea at all what it meant to have been gassed though we knew mustard gas was a Terrible Thing, had no idea that chlorine gas even existed, yet of course we came across and met a lot of people like that and we still had no imagination of the War, didn't really know anything about it, couldn't begin to think what it was like. When I went to Nottingham in 1952 Professor Pinto had all the first year English students round to his house one evening, he'd been in the Artists' Rifles and knew Siegfried Sassoon, but I never made the connection there either, when he showed us all his books inscribed by Sassoon and carefully paged through his big Max Beerbohm *Poets Corner*, talking about them and explaining them to us. The War was remote, his gentle reminiscences of the people he knew made it somehow a bit glamorous, the stuff of books really, and it was a real eye-opener the year I got my B.A., even if we had read a lot of poetry by Owen and Rosenberg and Sassoon, to look at a pictorial history of life on the Western Front which Frank Gibbon had brought from home, all those photos of damaged life in the trenches and death in the towns, bodies lying at the side of muddy roads.

Angus had a lot wrong with him not just his lungs, there were some things he couldn't eat, now and again Cook would make him something different, like herrings with mustard sauce, all bright yellow we thought it looked like custard only revolting instead of nice, and we'd watch him eat, lean over his food, "you put that on fish, Sir? *Eeyuew!*" He didn't really know how to talk to young boys and wasn't really at ease with us except when he could talk about painting and drawing and artists or show us how to do something, he cared enormously about that, and photography, he loved to encourage us and we responded to him he could always pick out the good bits of what you'd drawn or painted or modelled and he'd show you, make you feel pleased with what you'd miraculously done, he shared your distress if you'd worked hard at something and then it got ruined, somebody'd dropped a plaster-cast while moving it out of the way or torn a picture or spilled something on it or smudged their pastels. The Art Room was always an untidy dirty place, Nunc couldn't clean it properly, there was stuff spilled all over especially round the benches at the front, the gluepot always boiling over, there was a big grindstone on a wheel with its assorted litter in the corner, and pencil shavings scattered everywhere, it smelled of chalk and powdered posterpaint and gelatine, glue and plaster dust, crunchy underfoot, bits of string scattered round the place.

One year, this was quite a bit after the War, I must have been about twelve or thirteen, he did a whole series of ink drawings of some of the kids, he'd sent a note round to the parents, or Harry Brogden had, he was Headmaster then, offering to do portraits for a fee, I don't know how much they cost, about two pounds I suppose, he did one of me and another of Our Kid, Dad framed them in *passe partout* and taught me how to do it. I don't know what happened to those drawings, they must be around somewhere I suppose, the paper yellowing a bit, the ink bleeding a bit into its surround. Angus sat me in a chair in a storeroom he'd fitted up as a little studio and darkroom up above the Science Lab, he had a small easel and sketched me in pencil, I could hear his wheezy breath as he looked up at me and then back at the paper and he asked me what did my Dad do and what sort of a house we lived in and whether we went away for the summer holidays, did we go to the seaside, but I didn't say very much I couldn't think why he wanted to know these things I was sitting absolutely still I was afraid to move I didn't want to spoil the picture, Mum and Dad were paying for it, and he said "You don't have to sit still, you know. You can move your head about a bit and be comfortable," so I asked what would happen if I didn't get back to exactly where I was, "Won't you get it wrong, Sir?" and he grinned to himself and said "I know what you look like, you know, I see you often enough." I wondered why he needed me there at all then, and he said "I need to look at you closely to draw you properly, but you can relax a bit, there's no need to be so stiff" and after he'd drawn for a bit he said "so long as you don't keep fidgetting or wriggle about a lot." But he wouldn't let me see what he'd done at the end of the first session, it must have lasted about an hour and he said he wanted his tea, and he wouldn't let me see it at the end of the second session either but said, "No. I've got to do your brother next, and your mother and father should be the first to look at it, not you. I'm doing it for them, you know." When I did see it, after I got home for the holidays, I wasn't too pleased, my neck was all hunched down into my shoulders, but Mum said "Well you should have sat *properly.* It looks just like you, you nearly always sit like that." But I didn't like it as much as I liked the picture of Our Kid. But then Our Kid doesn't slump the way I do.

We knew nothing about him really except that he lived in the Lake District somewhere and went home for the holidays, one time this elegant middle-aged woman turned up at School dressed to the nines she looked much nicer than anybody's mum she looked like somebody posh in *Picture Post* or *Illustrated* asking for him and we all fell over when we found out it was his wife, some of us didn't believe it, "That's Mrs Angus?" we said, somehow that was hard to credit he was so scattered sometimes and untidy seeming. He was our HouseMaster his bedroom was across the corridor just outside the Second Dormitory, one winter we were all reading away under

the covers with our torches after Lights Out pools of light traversing
the ceiling a bit of whispering going on it was late he could see the
ceiling through the ventilators high on the walls and he called out
"Go to sleep! I can hear you, I'm not blind!" and then as he climbed
to the second floor on his patrol we heard him chuckle to himself
as he realised what he'd said and we all giggled our heads off. He
was often irked by us but it took a lot to make him lose his temper.
He couldn't bear the louts among us would call them lazy good-
for-nothings and once at dusk got so provoked by something Colin
Phelps did and said, I forget what but it had to do with how stupid
Art was, he said swear-words about Angus, Angus chased him
all wheezy and out of breath at top speed across the Quad and
up the belfry stairs where he'd forgotten there was a stair missing
and he really barked his shin, ripped a great strip of skin off, blood
everywhere, tore his trousers as his leg plummeted through the hole
and scraped against the splintered stair-edge *clunch!* and he cried
out, Colin got away. Angus wasn't quite sure who it was and was
bad-tempered for days after but we all sympathised with him not with
Colin because of what'd happened, it was funny but it was shocking.

The one with the real temper was Mrs Bailey. On Saturdays, right
after breakfast the dayboys all at home with their mum and dad
and us in the classroom all morning we had Mrs Bailey, nobody
else. She was far worse then than in the rest of the week, and after
Break at 11.00 she'd drill us in Mental Arithmetic. "This is the most
important subject you'll ever learn," she said, over and over, "you've
got to be quick, it's no good if you're slow! And you must never make
a mistake! *Never!*" and she'd fire questions at us, I'll never forget
the first day, like the other new boys I didn't know what we were
supposed to do. *You,* she said, *what's nine added to six? Quick now!*
and after a pause not even long enough to catch your breath *you're
too slow!* she hit her desk with the ruler. "I want to know *now*, right
now, now! you can't stop and think, you've got to do it *NOW!*" and
she turned to another boy, "What's twelve minus seven?" and waited
a second and shouted "Too late! You're too slow!" and she hit her
desk again, harder, and she turned to a kid in the front row and said
"Multiply eight by seven and a half!" The kid looked blank and she

hit his hand with her ruler, he flinched and went white, he didn't cry, and we all looked at him and quailed. "Sixty!" she cried, "Eight eights are sixty-four take away the four! Seven eights make fifty-six, add the extra four! You know your times-tables!" and we didn't dare look at her. As the class went on her face got redder and redder, she strode across the room and grabbed some child by the wrist, a barrage of *whack whack whackwhack**whack***, "You're just not trying! You're a very naughty boy." She looked at us all, "Why can't you get it right!" she shouted, "You're doing this on purpose! It's all very simple! You know your times-tables! We've done them in class, you've learned them." But of course we hadn't, not all our arithmetic books had them all the way up to eighteen-times, they stopped at twelve and most of them had pages missing or splodged illegibly with spilled ink, some pages in mine had bits missing and not just in the times-tables, and I had to copy out homework questions and all sorts of stuff into my Rough Book, someone had spilled so much ink onto my seven eight and nine-times that I couldn't read them any more than I could the ten-times, but that one was easy, all I had to do was count so there was nothing to learn, I didn't even have to think. We all copied the missing bits into our Rough Books, sometimes copying it down wrong, and as the book filled up I had to look harder and harder to find what I wanted, riffling through the increasingly tattered pages for my seven eight and nine times-tables. Perhaps that's why if I'm tired or have something on my mind I still get a bit hesitant or even confused where sevens or eights and nines multiply each other, I never really learned those stubborn factors but have to work them out. If I'm faced with "What's seven times nine?" the short-cuts in Mrs Bailey's mental arithmetic simply don't work for me, there's something too absurd about their devious ingenuity, they readily confuse addition with multiplication. Seven eights is fifty six, add nine and you get sixty-five, but that's hopelessly wrong. Start again, *seven sevens is 49*, twice nine is 18, *So add 20 and take away 2, 69 minus 2 is 67! Mrs Bailey would be proud of me!* But that's ridiculous! *7 x 10 is 70, take 7 away and you get 63. Aha! That's the right answer!* How could I be so dumb?

My real confusion in Mental Arithmetic and the times-tables was that I never could remember, when I was trying to work out the next figure in those fuzzy areas of the times-tables, that 7 x 9 is the same as 9 x 7. Sir William Rowan Hamilton, him of the quaternions, would've loved me for that, but Mrs Bailey had no interest in telling us how numbers actually work and probably had no idea, I suppose she never imagined that there's actually a word, *commutative*, to describe the way numbers behave in addition and multiplication where the answer's the same no matter what order you put the numbers in. I didn't know that word myself until I was well into adulthood, but we'd've loved a word like that, it would helped me anyway to remember, we all loved long words, we kept trying to learn new ones to baffle each other with, and of course it didn't matter if we nearly always got them wrong. How impressed we all were two or three years later when Henry Houston was giving out the books at the beginning of term in III A and asked us what sort of state they were in, most of them tattered and with loose pages but by-and-large complete, Ivor Williams stood up and said "Mine's indifferent, Sir" with a grin, I hadn't the faintest idea what it meant but it was such a lovely word, we all used it for weeks after, the way we learned to use "nondescript," mostly wrong.

Every now and again as soon as she came into the room Mrs Bailey told us to write out one of the times-tables *Do it right away!* we really did have to be quick, but it'd be all in front of your eyes as you did it so it was easier than reciting it straight off the bat, when you really did have to know. I can still remember a sunny winter morning a small fire in the fireplace writing the fourteen-times table. "This time you can do it in ink," she said, "It's time you started that. Take a page out of the middle of your Rough Book" and "Don't make any mistakes, you've got to be neat!" We got out our pens, I didn't know the fourteens table at all, I don't know that any of us did, I looked over at Adrian he was good at numbers he dipped his pen in his inkwell and started writing "1 x 14 =" "2 x 14 =" "3 x 14 =" and so on all the way to "14 x 14 =" down the left side of the page so I dipped my pen into the ink and started to do the same thing when I got to "2 x 14" I realised *oh! I can just add them up!* and I put down "28," *three times is twenty-eight and fourteen is forty-two, forty-two and fourteen is fifty-six, this is easy!* There were all sorts of little flecks in the paper shiny yellowish scraps of what looked like bits of straw your pen just skidded over them or a little string of curly thin hair, a tiny little scrap of wool likely, it'd catch in your nib you'd have to pull it off before it made a great big smudge, here and there spots of darker grey some of them printed letters we all knew

the paper we wrote on was made out of old newspapers and stuff it
was Wartime Paper made of Salvage it soaked up the ink in some
spots in some places it was thinner than tissue or even had a hole
in it you kept having to clean your nib off with a bit of paper you'd
torn off another page, none of us had any blotting paper *Ink rots
holes in your clothes*, Mum'd told me, and none of us'd ever heard
of anything like a paper towel or paper hankies. Ink was beginning
to get all over my fingers pale blue smears on the page *what would
Mrs Bailey think? what would she do?* it was cold, *she'll use that ruler
on me,* I shivered, don't make a mess, I dipped my pen in the inkwell
it picked up a great fat glob of muck from the bottom of the inkwell
a big fat blob fell onto the page a shiny wet blot of ink soaking into
the paper a little hill of sodden fluffy stuff in the middle and I looked
up Mrs Bailey was watching, her mouth sort of smirked a gash
of lipstick, she said "I think you'd all better start again, and use a
pencil," even Adrian had ink all over the place, everyone had ink all
over his fingers and on the page, there was sludge at the bottom
of everybody's inkwell we all picked some up on our nibs sooner or
later in big fat messy dripping clumps sometimes they just fell off the
nib as you moved your pen away from the inkwell or wouldn't scrape
off on the edge, you'd never want to get it back into the inkwell
anyway for you to pick up again another day, sometimes you could
wipe one off on a scrap of paper. John had blue streaks on his chin
and near his nose, he'd got some in his hair, "Neville, go round and
collect all the papers and put them in the wastepaper basket. And be
quick about it!"

But she wasn't often like that, she was too impatient, she
thought if *she* knew the answer *we* should know the answer, she
just made mental arithmetic too complicated, even now sometimes
I still think of something like twelve minus seven as *oh yes 2 plus 3
equals 5* and I have to sort out the convolutions that got me there,
the absolute rightness of ten as base. "How many pence in one
pound thirteen and sevenpence?" she'd ask, and we'd be stumped,
two hundred and forty plus twelve times thirteen plus seven, you
really did have to know your times-tables, and the intricacies of
money, "What's five pounds nine-and-eightpence from six pounds
twelve-and-tenpence?" They were impossible questions. Except
at Christmas and birthdays the most money we'd ever seen was
probably half-a-crown, I was nineteen before I ever saw a five-pound

note, that was at Nottingham we were going to the flicks at the Odeon and Brian Merrick had a five-pound note it was as big as a bedsheet we all clustered to get a look at it, they wouldn't take it at the box office even when he did know to sign it, *shades of Alice's wedding present!* it was enough to live on for a fortnight. At Brewood pocket money was thruppence a week, and the questions Mrs Bailey asked were completely meaningless. Later in the War, and after, we'd sneer at Americans and Canadians who had the simplicity of decimal money at their fingertips and floundered away at pounds shillings and pence, our secret pride in the best and proper way of doing things and knowing how it worked scorned the ease of their spending, in the War I heard a bloke in the bus say "Overpaid, oversexed and over here!" and laugh, not that it was funny, later on when we lived in Rugby it was a favourite complaint of Gordon Jones's , I didn't understand all that, though the derision in the laughter was clear enough.

But one Saturday in Mental Arithmetic Mrs Bailey said, pointing her ruler at Trevor, "Take four and sevenpence-three-farthings from eleven and sixpence-ha'penny. Quickly, now!" He went a bit pale and his face looked blank, and he said "Please Miss," and stopped. "What's the matter? she said, "It's just subtraction. Get on with it! *Do it in your head!*" She raised her ruler, and I looked away. She got to her feet and stepped between of the desks and my eyes dragged back. "*You,*" she said, her wool-skirted-figure hanging over him, "*Frank!*" he was one of the bigger boys, "Tell Trevor the answer. *Right now!*" and I recoiled a bit, thanking my lucky stars she wasn't looming over me, scared I'd cry if it was me. "I don't know, Miss," he said, in a small voice, "we haven't done fr–"and shut his eyes as she grabbed his wrist, lifted it high, *Whack!* Just once, hard, on the back of his hand, and then *Whack!* once more. A tear seeped from the corner of his eye. "*Haven't done what?*" she cried; "*your homework?* Why are you all such naughty boys?" The corner of her mouth turned down as she settled back to her chair. "Haven't done what," she said in a quiet voice, "Frank?" and he blinked, his eyelashes glistening in the light, "Fractions, Miss, we don't know how to do them." Mrs Bailey sighed, but even without farthings the questions didn't get any easier as the Term wore on. "How many pennies in thirty-eight shillings?" she'd bark, "That's nineteen times twenty-four! Quick, boy!" and if you took more than two seconds or came up with the wrong answer she'd take her ruler's edge to your knuckles, "Twice twenty-four is forty-eight times ten makes four hundred and eighty, take away twenty-four. *It's easy,*" she said, "You *must* try to please!"

Sometimes she'd start class by telling us "Arithmetic dictation. Write out these numbers." She sat at her desk, looked down at a piece of paper, read out a number. She only say it once and she watched to see that you wrote it down as she spoke, clear firm numbers. "Don't forget to be neat!" The first time she did it we thought it'd be easy, we all knew how many noughts there were in a million and even in a trillion, and she said "This is the first one. Two hundred and fifty-four" and we all wrote it down, and then she said "thousand" so we all put in a comma, and she said "one hundred and sixty-nine" and we all wrote it down and looked up, her nod of approval, watching, and she gave us the next number. It started out easy, but got harder and harder. "Next:" she said. "Four hundred and twenty-nine" she said, "million," she said, so I put in the comma, "Three hundred," she'd say, and I wrote down the "3" and looked up waiting for the rest, "and seventy two," and I wrote *that* down as with hardly a pause she said "Next, four hundred and ten thousand." We were all caught flat-footed, and most of us scrubbed away at that "372" we'd just written in thinking it was going to be three-hundred-and-seventy-two-thousand and tried to insert the three missing noughts. And she smiled and moved on to "six hundred and fifteen" and your paper became a real mess as she said "Next" and without a pause started a new number. You didn't dare stop writing, if you did she'd reach for her ruler and start out of her chair, still dictating, so you wrote down what you thought you remembered she'd said, trying to get hold of the next number, it was always a complicated one and you listened very hard while you tried to remember the one you'd missed. None of us ever got all the numbers right, and our pieces of paper were always messed up, great smudges from the india-rubber. "Why can't you simply write down the numbers?" she'd say, "just do what you're told?" and I suppose, looking back on it now, all these years later, that she thought she was teaching us to listen – to concentrate and remember – but it never occurred to her to tell us what she was doing or why she was doing it. How could we please her when she did what she did? Nobody escaped, and sooner or later no matter how hard we tried not to give in, we'd all've been crying *You're not trying hard enough!* welts on the bright

red backs of our hands, "You're being *deliberately* disobedient!"
Sometimes she drew blood, "Leave your hand alone, I didn't hit you
very hard! You've got to learn!" the back of your hand puffy and
bruised, so sore it hurt simply to ease your hand into your trousers
pocket. But it could start to get warm once you'd got it there.

    In the afternoons, when with all the other boarders we had
to go and watch one of the School soccer teams, we couldn't even
talk to each other about it, it was so different from home you couldn't
even begin to think about it, Mrs Bailey like the weather simply there,
just as unpredictable, you had to come up with desperate energy
and there weren't any answers, no-one to ask. It took most of the
weekend for your hands to recover, I don't know what the parents
of dayboys in Prep School must have thought but perhaps dayboys
didn't come on Saturday mornings I don't remember, at lunch some
kid down the table would see your hand as you reached for the
salt, say "Had Mrs Bailey this morning did you?" There'd be just the
boarders for lunch on Saturday juniors and seniors all mingled up
at the same table, everybody else gone home for the weekend, and
you'd remember it all again, everybody knew what was going on,
some of them would look up from their food or their conversation and
glance at you and look away, back to their chatter with their friends
while your cheeks suddenly felt a bit puffy and warm as you tried to
smile. I couldn't really look at anyone who'd been with me there with
Mrs Bailey, and they couldn't really look at me, we struggled to find
something to talk about, how the Wolves were doing or who had last
weeks' copy of the *Wizard*, but what talk we had simply petered out,
I felt ashamed of my crying, somehow the others knew too much
about me now, looked away at the merest glimpse of moisture round
someone's eyes, dreaded to notice, fought back whatever tears
welled up, blanked out the lively babble at the table, didn't listen.
It helped to think of Biggles and Algy and their heroics fighting the
Germans, but you knew that wasn't real, it was just a story, it didn't
stir the hollowness. By the end of the meal, though, some piece of
gossip, Basil Conrad sneaking out of the dorm late at night to go off
for a midnight bike ride and getting away with it, or Fargo Hopkins
somehow getting hold of an 1840 twopence-blue for his stamp
collection, pushed your troubled bewilderment underneath, pulled
you back into the world. After lunch you'd hold your hands under
cold water making the skin redder a touch of blue and you'd go and

watch the football game perhaps in the rain, you hadn't been able to dry your hands properly on the wet roller-towel behind the washroom door, a ring of wet round your shirt wrists, dank and uncomfortable, scuff your feet on the grass, your mac hanging down, clinging wet edge heavy against your bare legs.

But now and again on Saturday, and even during the week, starting in September 1942, my second year at Brewood, we'd go to class to find someone else there in her place, the awful knot of dread in your stomach diminished, the load of her punishments eased, released. What a sunny holiday when Mrs Asprey turned up, or Henry Houston, to teach us Arithmetic. Being in the classroom was different, completely changed. "John," she'd say, Mrs Asprey called us all by our first names, Mrs Bailey never did, "Campbell Minor" *she'd* say, or "Smith Major." Mrs Asprey would ask "How many pence are there in a shilling?" and John would say "twelve, Miss" in a faltering voice, making his answer sound like a question, and she'd smile and say "Yes, that's good" and "Henry, how many shillings in a pound?" and Henry would look relieved and say "Twenty, Miss" she'd smile again and say "Then what is twelve times twenty?" and we'd all chorus "Two hundred and forty, Miss" and feel pleased. "William," she'd say, and she'd smile, "it's not your birthday, is it?" and when he said "no, Miss" she said "Well, let's pretend that it is, and you just got a Postal Order for half-a-crown as a present and you've gone to Mrs Roberts's to buy some sweets for five of your friends. How much does a sherbet cost, you know the ones I mean, they come in a little packet with a liquorice straw, they're tuppence aren't they? So you've bought everybody a sherbet, and one for yourself, how many's that, six? How much change is Mrs Roberts going to give you?" and we all worked it out in our heads, it was easy even if she had got the prices wrong, they didn't cost *that* much, and just as William said "one-and-six" Henry said in a loud whisper, "a shilling, she'll keep sixpence" and Mrs Asprey suddenly looked stern but there was a sort of amused dimple in one corner of her mouth, "Are you calling Mrs Roberts a thief, Henry? You can't go round saying things like that about people" and he went red and mumbled "No, Miss, I was just making a joke" and she said "I know, but you shouldn't make jokes like that." Henry looked chastened, she didn't say another word but looked at Alf and asked him a question, she didn't put up with any nonsense and she wouldn't let you drift off into some sort of daydream, she was wonderful, if you were looking out of the window she'd call you back, or she'd come over to where you were and look out of the window too, to see what you were looking at and you had to say you weren't really looking at anything or you'd say "the rooks, Miss, they've found something" and she'd say "Yes but we're not here to look at rooks are we, you'd better try and answer the question. What was it?" and you didn't know of course so she'd have to tell you and you'd feel silly but you knew it was alright really, you could tell she enjoyed being with us she liked kids she didn't laugh much but she smiled a lot she wore the same sort of clothes our mums wore when they dressed up to go out somewhere, good wool tweeds or twinsets and what Mum called sensible shoes she was soft-looking and plump and Mrs Bailey was thin and hard and all sharp angles. Mrs Asprey lived in a great big house across from the village cricket ground, not that very much cricket was played there during the War, on our Sunday walks if we went down that way we'd look up the driveway and see the big shrubbery all dark green bigger than the one at Rushbury twice as dusty looking and the edge of a tennis court, we didn't dare go in it looked far too posh a place for that, much later on I was told that before the War she used to run a kindergarten school there, but there was no swank about it it wasn't at all splendid it looked lived in but quiet, prosperous, and private, a bit like Chillington Hall I suppose but of course a lot smaller, not the least bit grand the way Squire Giffard's was, his grounds went for miles, the big Avenue crossing the canal, we called the canal there The Cut, on a Private Bridge with fancy stone balustrades, the Park landscaped two hundred years ago by Capability Brown. He was the Chairman of the School Board of Governors and a magistrate, the only time you'd ever get to talk to him was when he came to the annual Speech Day at School, that was the only time you'd ever see him except at Church but you wouldn't talk to him there, a lean old man with a slight stoop who always wore a suit, he was a bit aloof though the villagers liked him he was the local gentry. Mrs Asprey wasn't like that but she had the same sort of class about her, it was in the way she walked and looked at you and spoke, I think her husband was a major or more likely a colonel away in the Army, somebody high up anyway, if it wasn't raining she'd come to School on her bike, it had a basket on the handlebars where she carried exercise books she'd taken home to mark, or she'd

walk, she liked exercise, but now and again she'd drive to School
in her car goodness knows how she got the petrol. Our Kid says
that when Frank Evans came back from the War he laughed at her
ignorance, said to his class that she didn't know any French at all,
'd been teaching the Third Form apostrophe-s, *Le fermier's vache*.
But I don't remember her ever showing anger, she'd get annoyed by
facetiousness and let you know she was irritated but she was always
soft-spoken and polite, she didn't have any doubt about anything
so far as we could see, she never shouted at us, she had a strong
sense of her position and what was proper, we always knew where
we were with her.

As 1942 stretched towards 1943 Mrs Bailey wasn't there as much
as she used to be, Mrs Asprey began giving us English lessons as
well as Arithmetic and one day she was standing there at the front of
the room, she didn't like to sit down much when she was teaching,
her right hand kept straying to her left wrist and then her left hand
would reach up to her throat and she stirred about a bit walked to
the window at the back of the room peered out towards the church
came back to the front looked up at us, her right hand back down to
her left wrist she sighed and she said "I can't see the church clock
but it's not working anyway. I haven't got my watch, does anybody
know the time?" and we all looked a bit puzzled, we none of us had
watches, Dad had said both Phil and me were far too young to have
a watch we'd only break them, they were hard to find anyway in the
War, you couldn't even get the pocket watches Marks and Spencer's
used to sell for five bob before the War, both Dad and Grandpa said
they were terrific, unconditionally guaranteed for a year, but *What
would a child do with a pocket watch anyway, besides lose it?* Not
many kids at School had a watch, not that we knew anyway, Dad
said they were only vulgar show-offs, you don't boast by giving your
children things like that, he'd say, that just *spoils* them, What do you
want a watch *for*? And there could be no answer to that question.
There weren't any clocks in public places so you didn't see one very
often, we knew what time it was because people told us what to do
or what time it was and she said "Who knows how to tell the time?"
and nearly all of us put a hand up it was a nice clear sunny morning,

a bit of a breeze, you needed a pullover if you were outdoors but better than in this stuffy room with all the windows shut small fire smouldering in the grate I wasn't at all sure I did know how to tell the time but I put my hand up with the others you didn't want to look ignorant, *I* didn't anyway, and I was pretty sure, the big hand said the minutes and the little hand the hours or was it the other way round, and I was waving my arm about but I didn't say anything, other kids were saying "I do, Mrs Asprey" and "Please, Miss," and she looked at me and she said "Peter, you go. Do you know which is my car? It's parked round the corner just by the Science Lab, it's the only one there," and I must have looked a bit doubtful as I stood up because she said "Are you sure you know how to tell the time? the big hand tells you the minutes and the little hand the hour" and I nodded and started to leave she said "Be as quick as you can. The clock is on the dashboard" and I said "Yes, Miss, just like on my Dad's car" and I clattered down the stairs and ran off, it was so good to be outdoors I was all excited at having a special task to do it was so nice to be moving about everybody else was in class the whole Quad was empty the sun shining on the red flowers in the centre flowerbed the Headmaster's front door was open somebody was shaking a rug out of a window upstairs in his part of the house dust and fluff flying out of a turbulence of blue and I suddenly got confused, *is it the little hand the minutes, it must be, hours are bigger than minutes, no the big hand moves quicker so it's the minutes the little one's the hours* and I couldn't remember which and then I was at the car I suddenly remembered I knew how to tell the time I opened the car door and I looked at the dashboard and it was covered with dials there were so many of them which was the clock? I couldn't find it, she did say it was on the dashboard didn't she but it wasn't there, in Dad's Austin it was right in the middle, a big dial, but not here, what was this, "Morris" it said, I looked on top of the dashboard but there wasn't anything there I climbed in the car and sat down in the driver's seat the dark leather was hot on the back of my legs it was all crackly a yellowy-brownish light coming through the speckled windows, they were made of layers of brownish glass lots of cracks and flat-looking loops all yellow peeling-looking it was just like the old car on the farm at Alcester a close dusty smell hot leather the car all closed up in the sun it was hot everything quiet I listened and there wasn't any sound at all somebody's voice droning through a window in the Science building there was a pair of soft leather gloves on the next seat a bit of screwed up brown paper and I looked and looked *Where was the clock?* all the dials looked the same everything was brownish and faded-looking the glass over the dials all dusty *Which one's the clock?* I could hear it ticking and suddenly there it was, right in front of my nose a small round disk just about an inch across, I had to count round the face the big hand was between the IV and the V and the little hand was past the XI and I climbed out of the car "*the little hand is past the eleven and the big hand is next to the five* it's nearly half-past eleven" and I closed the car door "*the big hand is nearly at the five and the little hand is next to the eleven* no no no it's the other way round it's nearly eleven thirty *the little hand is past the eleven and the big hand is next to the five* oh blimey which way round is it I can't remember" I rushed back to the car and peered through the window I couldn't see the clock clearly it was so gloomy in there so I opened the door again the handle hot on my hand as I pushed it down and peered in "I've been gone such a long time! she must wonder where I've been! she told me to hurry up! oh yes *the little hand's the eleven*" warm dusty air flowing out past my face smelling of car a mix of petrol and oil and dust and old scent and dry leather and I closed the door and ran like mad back to Rushall chanting *the little hand's just past eleven* over and over to myself a jingly little rhythm trying not to think *big hand* but knowing that I mustn't forget where it was and I got back, I stopped at the bottom of the stairs I walked carefully up at a proper pace Mrs Asprey didn't like noise and wanted us to walk properly everywhere but she had told me to hurry and I went in red-faced a bit sweaty and still out of breath I was sure she'd wonder why I'd been so long I'd been gone for ages I said "It's nearly half-past eleven o'clock, Miss" I was pretty sure I'd still got it right she'd be really cross if I hadn't but all she did was ask me where the hands were and I told her and she nodded and said "Oh, we've lots of time then, I thought it must be time to start English but we've a bit of time yet. Thank you Peter. Carry on, Patrick, tell me the answer" and she smiled so that was alright then and I went and sat down.

Henry Houston always knew what time it was, he was in charge of almost everything including telling people when it was Break, he'd send someone round from class to class to say it was Break, he was very stern, when he gave an address to the School

which he did sometimes at the end of Prayers he'd say *you rabbits*
or *you animals* in a fierce voice but you could tell he didn't mean it,
there was a twinkle of mock in his eye but he was still a bit fearsome,
he never promised a penalty he didn't give. He was always polite
and serious in class, scrupulously attentive, he explained things to
us as often as needed till we understood, he explained how Mental
Arithmetic works so we could do it, and it became a kind of game
but you'd better be attentive!, after he'd been teaching us for a while
we'd try to think out ways to do sums, short cuts, before he told
them to us. "If you have to multiply by nineteen do it by twenty and
then take one of them away; quick, what's nineteen times three?"
and he'd show us on the board, tell us "take away the three from the
sixty to get fifty-seven," and smile, if you got it wrong he'd simply say
"No. You took away nineteen instead of three. Try it again" but he'd
change the problem, "Twenty-seven times four" and see if you made
the same mistake, urging you to be quick, friendly, attentive, he
made it a bit of a contest so that sometimes we'd actually get almost
to enjoy it, ask how you did it, we weren't terrified, we wanted to win,
but he wasn't pleased if you kept making the same mistake. "Think,
you rabbit!" he'd say lifting one eyebrow. We adored him, he was
all bark and only bit if you deserved it, his bit had *bite*, his ability to
lift one eyebrow much higher than the other terrified and fascinated
us we quailed before it, he told us he'd been injured when he was a
young man in the 1920s in hospital his head in bandages for months
his right eyebrow immobilised he didn't say more except that was
why he could lift the left one so high. It all sounded heroic, for weeks
after that you'd see troops of small boys going round the School
with one hand pressed firmly over one side of their face wiggling
the visible eyebrow furiously up and down, we did it everywhere we
went, we practiced and practiced but it didn't make any difference
none of us ever learned how to do it, I didn't anyway. The villains
in all the stories we read, like the Nazi air ace Eric von Stahlhein
in *Biggles Flies West* or General von Scharnkamf or whatever his
name was of the Gestapo in the *Wizard*, always had a supercilious
look on their face when they shot a plane down or tortured prisoners
or even talked to underlings, that's how we knew they were villains,
enemy spies were called supercilious so we'd know they were spies,
and the craze for wiggling one eyebrow and not the other came to a
sudden stop when one of the older boys, I think he was in the Fourth

Form, told Harold that *cilia* was Latin for eyebrow and *supercilious* meant raising one eyebrow higher than the other, "Why d'you want to look like a Nazi?" he scoffed, "That's bonkers." But of course you still raised your eyebrows, you can't stop doing that, and I still have a sneaking regard for people who can lift just one, wish I could do it, Phil still does it, beautifully, when he wants to look at you askance, it's terrific for dealing with kids, scornful and slightly comic all at once.

       Henry wouldn't ever put up with nonsense and he never lied to us, when I was about twelve he spent a whole Geography class telling us what we were like inside, telling us how vulnerable to serious damage the bladder was when full, how it distends, little drawings on the blackboard, I haven't the faintest idea if they were even remotely accurate, "And if you ever raise your hand and ask to be excused to go to the bathroom I never say no. Now you know why." What a change from Mrs Bailey, we never abused that, he trusted us, he helped us cope he helped us recover, he must have known what was going on, but he was only the Assistant Headmaster and she was the Headmaster's Wife, I see now that she must have been a very unhappy woman and by the end of 1942 she must have been a worried woman, very worried indeed, but he'd try to cheer us up, he'd talk to us while we watched the game on Saturday afternoon, he talked to us outside class or if he came across us in the village or on our Sunday Walks. But I never was able to like Arithmetic. I must have found it quite easy at first because at Christmas 1941 I got 72% for the first Term's work and 100% in the exam, in the second it wasn't so good, with 38% in the Term and 100% in the exam and at the end of the year, Summer Term 1942, I was terrible, I got 27 and 50, Mrs Bailey wrote "Moderate" and when I came back in September my marks were even worse, 36% for the Term and only 30 in the exam, "More effort required, DCB." My marks began to improve once Mrs Asprey got to be our regular Teacher, and by the time I finished my second year in Prep School I was ranked 3rd in the class. But by then we didn't see Mrs Bailey very much even though she still wrote up our Reports. We didn't know it, but she had her own troubles.

Melchior Vischer's
Second through Brain
On Translating the First Dada Novel*

David Vichnar

> Only randomly does one peek into life. Perhaps my life was just a life lived
> in-between experiencing. Perhaps I haven't lived a life at all,
> perhaps it was the life of another, or a life that no-one's ever lived.

He was only twenty-seven when he wrote this postscript to his third and most autobiographical novel, *Der Hase*—a strangely prophetic/ proleptic formula that the eighty-odd years his own life eventually amounted to were supposed to exemplify. Not that he could have had any reason to suspect at this stage the future downward spiral into anonymity and non-existence those years would indeed become. For in 1922, Melchior Vischer was gaining acclaim as the pioneering representative of the dada movement in Prague, which was to materialise a year later in the honourable mention from the committee of the highly prestigious Kleist Prize. His early publications had received excellent reviews, and his fame as a writer was further enhanced by his reputation as a newspaperman and essayist, and also an early champion of Franz Kafka, Franz Werfel, and Robert Musil.

---

* This essay is a version of "Radiantly Splattered: Melchior Vischer's *Second through Brain*," my introduction to the translation of this first dada novel. The translation is the work of Tim König and myself and was published by Equus Press in 2015.

Although only slightly younger than these more famous Prague-German authors, Vischer was to outlive them all by more than three decades, the only one to survive the Second World War. But longevity came at a price: his death in Berlin, in 1975, concluded decades of obscurity; an obscurity as complete as it was mysterious—the product, variously, of a failed artistic vision and what in the end was his highly elusive, taciturn personality. Vischer's obscurity became so complete, in fact, that when a year after his death his juvenilia of the early 1920s was being reprinted for the very first time, the publisher was unable to trace the copyright holders.

"A LIFE OF ANOTHER": EMIL FISCHER & MELCHIOR VISCHER
Born Emil Walter Kurt Fischer, Melchior Vischer (1895-1975)[1]—as he came to be known—was the son of an apothecary in Teplice, a spa town in the Sudeten region of North-West Bohemia. He was just old enough to complete his secondary education at a Prague grammar school before the outbreak of World War I—into which he was promptly enrolled, serving as a lieutenant in a Hungarian infantry regiment stationed in Galicia. The end of the First World War found Vischer in Prague, recovering from a neck-injury received on the front. After recuperating he enrolled at Charles University and took a position at the newly formed *Prager Presse* as a theatre-critic. It was in this post that he met the actress Eva Segaljewitsch, of a Jewish origin, whom he soon married.

And it was also during this period that Vischer made his notable debut on the international literary scene, with the publication, in 1920, of *Sekunde durch Hirn* (*Second through Brain*), and from his mid- to late-twenties, Vischer's star continued to rise, publishing a further three novels and a variety of novellas and short stories,[2] all of which garnered high praise within Prague German literary circles. Critic Johannes Urzidil described Vischer's *Second through Brain* as

---

[1] The following account is loosely based on Peter Engel's entry on Vischer in *Prager Profile: Vergessene Autoren im Schatten Kafkas*, ed. Hartmut Binder (Berlin: Binder, 1991); on Hartmut Geerken's "Afterword" to *Melchior Vischer, Sekunde durch Hirn, Der Teemeister, Der Hase und andere Prosa* (München: Hartmut Geerken, 1976); on Jürgen Serke's *Böhmische Dörfer—Wanderungen durch eine verlassen literarische Landschaft* (Wien, Hamburg: Paul Zsolnay Verlag, 1987); and most crucially, on Christian Jäger's *Minoritäre Literatur. Das Konzept der kleinen Literatur am Beispiel prager- und sudetendeutscher Werke* (Wiesbaden: Deutscher Universitäts-Verlag, 2005).

[2] In addition to *Sekunde durch Hirn* (*Second through Brain*, 1920), the most prominent are *Strolch und Kaiserin* (*Tramp and Empress*, 1921), *Der Teemeister* (*The Teamaster*, 1921) and *Der Hase* (*The Hare*, 1922).

the literary equivalent of a Cézanne's canvass – an exploration of spatial form by the temporal means of narrative.[3] The Brno-born Ernst Weiß, reviewing *Second* for *Das Tage-Buch*, spoke of Vischer's dada as a "poetic form":

> In every line of this extraordinary work there's the effortless gift of grace: poetry [...]. A second through brain, a dreamsecond through the brain of a man deliriously falling, the metamorphoses of Venus, the thousand faces of the earth spirit, heads and their contraries experienced at a thousandmile tempo, sucked away by an overpowering drive for being [...]. Dada is a form, Dada itself is a form for a poet.[4]

In 1923, at the apogee of his literary career, Vischer abandoned his post at the Prager Presse and departed from the city to spend four years fruitlessly wandering through Germany in pursuit of a career in the theatre. In 1927, Vischer finally settled in Berlin, seeking to establish himself in the German capital as a playwright—a decision he came to regret more than once. By the early 1930s, unable to make ends meet penning theatre reviews on the side, Vischer turned his hand to writing popular sensational novels, which he penned in tandem with his wife Eva.

For some, this is where the story of Melchior Vischer ends, the rest being at best an embarrassed silence. Bibliography and biography agree on one point: that the name Melchior Vischer didn't survive the 30s, for in 1940 and 1942, he reinvented himself yet again as a children's author, publishing two "Indian" adventure books under the name Emil Fischer. This reversion to his birth name (itself often taken for a pseudonym: his name, just as his life, having meanwhile become that "of another") signaled a turning point in Vischer's already chequered career, and accounts of the succeeding years vary significantly depending upon the source. As with everything, these years were overshadowed by Hitler's war in Europe, but if one is to believe Hartmut Geerken, editor of the 1976 reprint of Vischer's juvenilia, there was an especial poignancy in the coincidence of Nazi Germany's rise and impending downfall with that of Vischer the writer, whose ambitions now tended towards the historical:

---

[3] Qtd in Jäger, *Minoritäre Literatur*, 465.

[4] Qtd. in Serker, *Böhmische Dörfer*, 165.

The beginning of a Thousand-Year Reich and the exhaustion of Vischer's creative accomplishments seem to overlap in time. Vischer was to become a writer of histories. Two voluminous historical biographies, on Burkhard Münnich (1938) and Jan Hus (1940), carry him, together with a few youth books, through the Third Reich.[5]

Following the death from cancer in 1943 of his wife (whom, writes Engel, he had refused to divorce despite her being a Jew), Vischer soon re-married—a certain Margot Jorcyk, 20 years his junior but already with three children of her own. This second marriage having quickly fallen apart, Vischer's poverty reached hitherto unparalleled proportions, and he found himself, more than once, reduced to begging. It was at this point, three decades after abandoning Prague, that Vischer suddenly began remembering his long-gone friends from the '20s and turned to them for help. Only one of them—Urzidil, now an émigré in New York—responded to Vischer's desperate pleas, sending him some sort of allowance, this despite Vischer's status as "a man mistrusted by many émigrés for having stayed in Nazi Germany."[6] As the enormity of the error in forsaking and disavowing his Prague/Sudeten heritage started to dawn on him, Vischer wrote to Urzidil: "Only now have I understood: Prague is not Berlin; Berlin is exile!"[7] But Urzidil's support only went so far, and didn't last long. Once more facing poverty, Vischer refashioned himself again and turned to producing a body of religious poetry—in Engel's generous estimation, of "no match for his early output."[8] Having thereby completed a metamorphosis from literary revolutionary to anonymous hack, and after more than two decades of living off social security benefits, Emil Fischer/Melchior Vischer died on 21 April 1975, in a suburb of West Berlin.

MELCHIOR VISCHER/EMIL FISCHER
No. 2948559

It would be easy to let the story lie there, strange and often incomprehensible as it is. Both Engel and Geerken do so, avoiding the blanks, omissions and contradictions that so obviously mar Vischer's

[5] Geerken, "Nachwort," 192.

[6] Serke, *Böhmische Dörfer*, 163.

[7] Qtd. in Serken, *Böhmische Dörfer*, 181.

[8] Engel, *Prager Profile*, 417.

biography. History is easily the first suspect to blame for much of the absurdist undercurrent in this story, but passing the buck to it would just be so much sentimental whitewash, as Christian Jäger's recent and highly detailed *Minoritäre Literatur* demonstrates. Rereading Vischer's biographies from 1938 and 1940, alongside a trove of archival material (made available at the Berlin Bundesarchiv only after the re-unification of Germany), Jäger arrives at a very different story.

It begins on 1 May 1933, when Vischer applies to become "a member of NSDAP" (the Nazi Party) and is subsequently registered at "the Starnberg party office under member number 2948559." This decision, Jäger shows, is no temporary lapse of reason or merely self-protective measure, for in his relationship with Nazism Vischer is quite proactive. In autumn 1938, Vischer published a monumental biography of Burkhard Christoph von Münnich, the 18th-century field marshal and military reformer who served Tsarina Anna of Russian, under the title *Münnich. Ingenieur / Feldherr / Hochverräter* (*Münnich: Engineer / Commander / High Traitor*). Vischer's biography hinges on a "case study" of the clash between German militarism (exemplified by Münnich) and Russian "backwardness," "cowardice," and downright "insanity," ultimately depicting "military putsch and military dictatorship as ethical commands" and "the soldierly Führer-state as the last hope."[9] The entire work effectively serves to vindicate the expansive war politics of *Drang nach Osten* even before it actually came into practice. Little wonder, then, that the Office for Literature Services, through a statement made by the Cultural-Political Archive of the Reich's Culture Ministry, found the manuscript "of very good quality and recommendable."[10]

Vischer's second biography, on the "life and time" of Jan Hus, turns out to be a piece of rabid Czechophobic propaganda. The fact that Jan Hus was born during the rule of Charles IV, who also happened to be the Holy Roman Emperor (thus ruling over parts of Germany as well), appears to have been license enough for Vischer to turn him into a "Sudeten German [...] who carries out the genetic programme of his bloodline."[11] Hus, who only wrote in Latin and/or Czech (a language Vischer himself never had any decent command of) and on some highly learned and abstract subjects, is deintellectualised

---

[9] Jäger, *Minoritäre Literatur*, 485-7.

[10] Jäger, *Minoritäre Literatur*, 489.

[11] Jäger, *Minoritäre Literatur*, 493.

and "Germanised" into an anarchic, folkloric instigator of popular uprisings, very much in the vein of the later Thomas Münzer. The worst about Vischer's biography is not that it's factually distorted and propagandistic, but that it caricatures the unlawfully persecuted saint (and Czech national symbol) as "a leftist radical, an anarchist inciter, who not only was condemned rightfully, but even was himself to blame for his own downfall" and seeks, under the pretext of historical biography, to vindicate Nazi foreign policy.

Added to this is Jäger's discovery in the Berlin Bundesarchiv that Vischer's membership application to the Nazi Writers' Association in August 1938 refers to the decision of the "C2 Berlin District Court" which has "divorced" marriage to his Jewish wife Eva German, and a tawdry and sadly commonplace 20th-century Mitteleuropean tale seemingly becomes complete: "Even before the so-called seizure of power, [Vischer] was on the Nazi path, instigating and currying favour, forecasting the future military Führer-state and abusing its enemies; he was a veritable fighter for the Thousand-Year Reich."[12] Jäger leaves it at this, failing to provide any proof of extant divorce papers or detailing Eva German's final years. One can imagine a scenario in which Vischer's application may have been a red herring to the authorities, an attempt at currying favour during particularly harsh times, without actually betraying his, by all accounts, beloved first wife – but that is where history turns into conjecture and fiction, so the rest should be, as indeed it was in Vischer's case, silence.

In view of this serial metamorphosis—of Melchior Vischer the Prague Dadaist (1920) into No. 2948559 at the Starnberg NSDAP office (1933) into Emil Fischer the distortionist, populist and demagogue historian (1940)—the tale of Vischer's post-war reticence and self-imposed exile loses much of its mystery. It becomes less a story of literary historical injustice as of a culpable disavowal of past political incriminations and evaded consequences: the "life of another," as for so many former collaborators and apologists of Nazism, offering that most banal means of escape from the perils of one's own.

FROM F TO V & BACK, OR: WHAT'S IN A NAME

But how exactly did Emil Fischer turn into Melchior Vischer in the first place? Why did he leave Prague at the height of his fame, just one year before the birth of Poetism, the first genuinely Czech avant-

---

[12] Jäger, *Minoritäre Literatur*, 503.

garde movement? Why, as a dada novelist of some renown, did he turn to theatre adaptations and to second-rate popular novels? And is there anything about his early-20s Prague sojourn that would help explain the subsequent U-turn in Vischer's national(ist) and political affiliations?

"Melchior Vischer" first came into being in a letter dated 29 December, 1918, addressed to Tristan Tzara, the "dada papa," in which Fischer/Vischer described himself as "an expressionist of the utmost left," hastening to add that "against Dadaism I take up no hostile attitude."[13] Dada reached Prague soon after the end of the First World War: in September 1919 a student magazine announced a dada journal to be launched by a group of young Czech poets. In March 1920, Raoul Hausmann and Richard Huelsenbeck staged two dada evenings in Prague. However, the plans of forming a Prague Dada group never quite panned out: the announced dada journal never actually took off, and the group around it was in all respects ephemeral. It was only in the mid-1920s that Prague's preoccupation with dada reached any systematic, programmatic level—and by that time, Vischer had already become a Berlin-bound nomad.

Still, unsurprisingly, Prague's first documented reactions to dada took place in the German-speaking community. Vischer's correspondence with Tzara points out that Prague German newspapers reported on dada as early as the summer of 1918, which for Vischer the newspaperman was a prime source of information. The new movement, he notes with surprising dejection, was greeted rather suspiciously. "First of all: one is against dada,"[14] wrote Vischer in the first letter, from 29 Dec 1918 and detailed an atmosphere of pettiness and hostility toward Expressionism and dada on both the German and Czech sides, illustrating thereby that "Prague public clearly has no interest whatsoever" in it. In a letter from March 1919, indifference grew into mockery: "In this country, it is considered part of tasteful journalism to sneer at Dada."[15]

One has little more than Vischer's word for it—this was a correspondence between one radical writer and another, who was trying to establish an alliance in a common fight against enemies of new directions. Even stranger is Vischer's sentiment that the general

[13] Vischer, *Unveröffentlichte Briefe und Gedichte,* ed. Raoul Schrott (Siegen, 1988) 5.

[14] Vischer, *Unveröffentlichte Briefe,* 4

[15] Vischer, *Unveröffentlichte Briefe,* 5.

public should somehow be *in favour of* Dada, or in other words, that dada should pave a direct path to popularity. His letters are peppered with exaggerated claims of having elicited "public uproar" and "scandal" with his own assaults upon public taste, such as must have elicited a certain amusement from the founder and manager of the Cabaret Voltaire.

Side by side with these laments, Vischer bewailed his lack of direct access to dada writings. "I'd therefore be really interested," he wrote, "to know something more than just the names Tzara, Arp, Picabia, Janco, Giacometti, Huelsenbeck etc.,"[16] asking Tzara to kindly send his way any dispensable dada-related articles, brochures, prospects and sample magazine issues. A year later (in January 1920) Vischer wrote again, this time with the manuscript of his "Merzroman" aka *Sekunde durch Hirn* (an allusion to Kurt Schwitters's "Merz" collages), inquiring if the dada papa couldn't be tempted to read it. Just how in/active Tzara was in responding to Vischer is brought home by the fact that only once over the course of eight letters does Vischer thank Tzara for a reply "note." Vischer had even enclosed a 35-cent postage stamp with his manuscript, which to Schrott's mind "makes quite plausible the conclusion that Tzara was delaying the correspondence, as the outrageous tone of Vischer's letters had prompted him to regard Vischer as not exactly a promising fellow traveller."[17]

The Paris/Zürich/Berlin dada axis, for the Vischer of 1920, evidently presented a more international—and thus more apposite and advantageous—artistic worldview than the Prague offshoot of German expressionism. Vischer's expectations from his dada alignment were nothing short of earth-shattering: in a French salutation to Tzara and Picabia from April 1920, Vischer announces the publication of *Sekunde* as no less than "a bomb which has to burst open with infection the skulls of our dear 'bourgeoisie,'" and promises to set the world on fire with it. The wish/reality discrepancy is close to poignant. While assuring both that "*Second* is the first Dada-novel and must march triumphantly [...] across Europe," Vischer still has the need to beg for their interest: "I beg of you to kindly take interest in my novel [...] and please send me three copies each of every critique."[18]

As his rather one-sided correspondence with Tzara suggests,

[16] Ibid.

[17] Vischer, *Unveröffentlichte Briefe*, 14.

[18] Vischer, *Unveröffentlichte Briefe*, 7.

Vischer's avant-garde affiliations, just as by now almost everything else about his "life of another," were tenuous at best. Vischer's change from F to V, from an "Expressionist" in 1918 to a Dadaist in 1920 to a dropout in 1923 (and whatever followed afterward) should be seen in the context of the political changes in the Central Europe of that period. Born into, for all intents and purposes, a German-speaking country, after the 1918 establishment of Czechoslovakia, Vischer found himself a member of an ostracised (and in reaction radicalised), dwindling language-minority. It certainly wasn't Vischer's decision to fight in the war—even less so, on the losing side—nor was it his choice to end up as a war casualty in Prague, a city in which he felt increasingly alienated and isolated. And it seems there are grudges held in Second, for no other city (not even Vienna) gets quite as harsh a treatment as this "yellowed funnel by the plagued canopy bed Europe":

> The city of howler monkeys & fleas, of corruption, of the New-European bacillus idioticus militaris, also the crucial point of all the pennons of an occidental world with arsphenamine treatment, head office of pushers, who hustled bull market with state insolvency, of clogged sewerage, of the fastest streetcar in the world & the city of six thousand ministers. Everybody is, has been or shall be, a minister. In exchange for that the nation's splendidly off. (82)

Given that Vischer spoke no Czech, his envisaged plan of a Prague dada franchise may not have been as opportunistic as most commentators would have it. Under the cultural and linguistic policy of the new Czechoslovak state, Vischer and scores of his Prague-German compatriots were becoming increasingly marginalised. By 1923, with Second through Brain failing to "march triumphantly across Europe," its author instead undertook the marching himself.

"A BOAT RIDE OVER THE NIAGARA"

Second through Brain appeared in 1920 at the Steegemann publishing house, in the dada series called "Die Silbergäule" ("The Silverhorse"), with a cover design by Kurt Schwitters. Upon its publication, *Second through Brain* was promoted as the first "dada novel" – "insofar," as Vischer himself wrote in a January letter to Tzara, "as one can still use the silly word 'novel' at all."[19]

    Vischer's narrative consists of a series of disconnected

---

[19] Vischer, *Unveröffentlichte Briefe*, 6.

vignettes, flashing through the mind of one Jörg Schuh, a stuccoist in the process of falling off the scaffolding of a fortystorey construction site. Staring certain death in the eye, the protagonist embarks on a cab ride "on the great Milky Way" which takes him through his past life, both actual and also the many might-have-beens. Although the setting of Jörg's fall has no place name proper, most of the flashbacks do have a local habitation: his conception at a Central-European brothel and his birth aboard an Andalusian barge in the Lisbon harbour give rise to a highly erratic, if also very place-specific travelogue. Throughout, Jörg appears in different times, spaces and impersonations: he witnesses his own conception through a union between a negro pagan and central-European prostitute, he experiences his prenatal life, his birth, his existence as a newborn, and an interminable series of further careers/incarnations: an athlete, excavator-driver, carver, fake monk, stonemason, grammar-school pupil, footballer, Eskimo, a "president of America," a coolie in Japan, a lecturer on political economy in an African "Caoutchoucstate," a rat in Beijing, a "man in the moon," a Jew-killing minorite priest, president of Germany, then back to the falling Jörg Schuh and, finally, a "brain radiantly splattered" (100) against the pavement. This fantastic roller-coaster ride through the head, in turn, takes Jörg from Genoa, St. Gotthard, and Vienna, to "a thermal city in which Goethe had stayed temporarily" (i.e. Vischer's native Teplice) and onwards: to Lapland, Nagasaki, Notre Dame, "Caoutchoucstate, Africa," Shandong, the Moon, Prague, Madrid, Fiume, Budapest, Berlin, Brazil, Cape Horn, Chicago, and toward the great beyond.

Apart from using some of the typical Dadaist stylistic techniques as visual typography, non-lexical onomatopoeia, meta-narration, and textual montage, *Second through Brain* also seeks to programmatically align itself with the Zürich/Berlin dada group. There is, famously, the "intertelluric greeting to Serner and Tzara," with the prospect of "a boat ride over the Niagara" (74)[20]—emblematic of the movement's zany shock tactics and almost self-sacrificial measures to which it resorted. These are brought into relief in this crucial passage:

> Do you think me crazy? Oh no! it's only my environment that's moronic, civilised, besmeared, hence me the oddball. Especially odd the superpious healthy fat folks & gym teachers. We want to smash culture into pieces, also the bourgeois madness, which is

[20] All translated quotations from *Sekunde durch Hirn* are taken from Melchior Vischer, *Second through Brain*, trans. David Vichnar & Tim König (Prague: Equus Press, 2015).

so often nicely lacquered and bound in Morocco leather, we're heading out all the way to the utmost end, bordering on the big freedom: ur-being. We rubble, we rubble, & if da da, from the ground up, at first cringed lacquered speech, then the only thing remaining now would be the whole big DADA.—Here's to you, Huelsenbeck, Baader & Schwitters. We have no pity. We show saneness & whoa common sense from its downside. (97)

In this programmatic statement, Vischer's disparagement and critique of the perceived "bourgeois madness" and the "lacquered language" of his contemporaries fits the bill (almost to a fault) of all the four major phases in the social roles assumed by the avant-garde, identified by Renato Poggioli in his seminal *The Theory of the Avant-Garde*.[21] The first of these, *activism*, refers to the avant-garde taste for action and agitation for the sake of agitation, and the pleasure derived ("We have no pity"). From this activism directed at anyone and no-one ("the superpious healthy fat folks" as well as "gym teachers") follows a more general social attitude of the avant-garde termed *antagonism*. *Nihilism* is the third, destructive phase manifest in the work of the Dadaist ("we rubble, we rubble"), issuing into *agonism*,[22] the pathos and suffering of the artist/victim/hero—chiming well with Vischer's desire "to smash culture into pieces, also the bourgeois madness." A case in point, then, of dada ideology if not technique? Indeed, it is the textbook, clichéd character of proclamations such as this that challenge the extent to which *Second through Brain* is dada in its actual poetics rather than mere wish-fulfilling agenda.

"A SHROVETIDE PLAY"

The when and how of Emil Fischer's metamorphosis into Melchior Vischer having been established, the question still remains: why? Jäger[23] offers as good and educated a guess as any, suggesting it served a double purpose, assuaging his Catholic upbringing in the face of what were admittedly unorthodox artistic aspirations, while also acting as the vehicle for their embodiment. "Melchior" quite plausibly refers to one of the so-called three magi—whose feast (the epiphany) falls onto 6 January, a near overlap with Fischer's own birthday—and

---

[21] Renato Poggioli, *The Theory of the Avant-Garde*, trans. Gerald Fitzgerald (Camridge MA & London: Harvard University Press, 1968).

[22] Cf. Poggioli, *The Theory of the Avant-Garde*, 22-30; 61-2.

[23] Jäger, *Minoritäre Literatur*, 459.

"Vischer" seems related to the brass-founder and church sculptor Peter Vischer (the Elder), who died on 7 January 1529. Vischer's penchant for the charms of "kingship" would of course, later on, rear its ugly head during the seductions of Nazism, but the Christian resonance of his artistic pseudonym is of more direct interest for a debut text like *Second through Brain* with its concluding reference to "censers" and a prominent typographic image of the cross.

Second through Brain presents a special kind of iconoclastic text in refusing to undermine the dogma and expose the ridiculousness of organised religion, but reduces its critique to drawing upon Catholicism's own tradition of misrule and the carnivalesque. The text's programmatic "Pro- and Epilogue," classifies *Second through Brain* generically as a "Shrovetide play" (Fastnachtspiel, 51), placing it in the tradition of excessive merry-making prior to the forty-day period of Lent fasting (Fastnacht literally refers to the eve of the fast). Equally significant for the Catholic dimension of Vischer's text is that regulating the Shrovetide unruliness was the institution of confession: before embarking on the merrymaking, all ye faithful were expected to be "shrived," i.e. absolved from their confessed sins. The ensuing carnival would, over the course of centuries, blend theatrical and sporting events, performances of masques vying for the good believers' attention with games of football. Apart from participating in the "Shrovetide" tradition of festive misrule, *Second through Brain* is also steeped in Catholic tradition by "making it new" largely through parodying the old, which the modern cannot plausibly do without. On one of his journeys, Vischer's protagonist is caught "thinking of Thomas Aquinas, then of Grünewald, at last of Gauguin" (86), arriving at modernity only via mediaeval scholasticism and gothic expressionism. The sense of traditionalism, of conservatism, underlying much of *Second through Brain*, is brought home towards the end, the only identification mark of the protagonist's corpse being his "oddly pushed-in shuteyes, as in ancient Egyptian mummies" (100).

What the Shrovetide did to the medieval conception of time (stopping it dead for a whole week), space (collapsing its everyday boundaries) and social identity (reversed and deranged, the holy profaned and the profane hailed), Vischer's *Second through Brain* does to narrative. It freezes its temporal duration, collapses its spatial boundaries, and lampoons its habitual realist underpinnings. These vignettes, as the text's subtitle has it, are "freakily high-torqued" before

Jörg's/the reader's eyes, until reach the ground he finally does, landing "on the plaster of smashed heads & necks" (99). His corpse gets collected for inspection at the clinic and ends up blessed, just as the text itself, with a final cross, to the accompaniment of "swinging censers" (100). The historical time in which the narrative is set is referred to only obliquely, through several allusions to contemporary sociopolitical matters. Vischer's Prologue only mentions that the manuscript was "written in Prague at a time so molluscan I cannot really determine it mathematically" (51) and almost all of Jörg's shenanigans take place in a perfect timeless simultaneity where Pythagoras coexists with Hedwig Courths-Mahler, a turn-of-the-century proto-feminist writer.

JÖRG SCHUH'S DADASEIN

A consistent (and unfortunately untranslatable) pun throughout Vischer's text lies in the homophony between dada and "da, da" ("there, there" in German). And yet, in the episodic, disjointed, and radically plural narrative of *Second through Brain*, the protagonist is never quite "there," his identity, just as his whereabouts, always likely to undergo a complete change, paragraph by paragraph.

So breakneck is the speed of these changes that Jörg himself has difficulty keeping up, as when he "wondered about the sudden spatula in hand, which traversed untoward crannies through the wood" and only later "remembered that yesterday, having been picked up on the street [...] he'd promised to learn god-carving" (62). Again, it's not so much the what as the how that's new: Vischer's narrative is a 20th-century energised, and supersized version of the long German picaresque tradition on fast-forward, extending all the way back to Grimmelshausen's *Simplicius Simplicissimus* or the folkloric Till Eulenspiegel cycle. Also, Jörg's opening encounter with the "Milky Way cabman" in "a specular tophat" alludes to Faust's meeting with Mephistopheles, especially since Jörg's first desired destination is the brothel (54). Similarly to these literary precursors, Vischer's Jörg Schuh is a "onedimensional" man, whose raison d'être is the fulfilment of the basic physical needs: hunger after food, need for pleasure, and desire of power and fame.

This projects into the conjoined themes of the text's gender- and race-politics. Jörg Schuh's "dadasein," so to speak, subscribes to some deep-rooted conventions and stereotypes, however, not without some effort on Vischer's part to undermine them. It's true Vischer does go along with them for quite a while: throughout, women appear as sexual objects to be used and discarded by the ever-horny protagonist. Although the protagonist's fatal fall is caused by his eyeing "the huge bosom of maid Hanne from the skyscraper opposite no. 69" (53), this does not seem to deter him from giving free rein to what could be diagnosed as full-blown Don Juanism. From the first encounter with a woman called Rahel, Jörg's one and only "talent & strength" (60) is his lust after, and capability of, superhumanly satisfying legions and legions of women, which reduces whatever possible character motivation and psychology he might possess to that of an itinerant male member. The only woman with some backstory, and the only one Jörg deigns to marry, is "Miss DDr. Bathseba Schur" ("Shearer"), whose "braininess"—two doctorates in medicine and philosophy at the tender age of 24—apparently renders her unwomanly, a specimen of "exceptional manwomanhood" (69). For Vischer, the dada revolution was evidently not fought for female emancipation, nor, for that matter, was the "Jewish question" among its interests: when Bathseba dares to "circumcise her new, oh so mighty husband" (71), Jörg gives her a mighty slap and takes to flight.

The same goes for racial stereotyping. The translation replicates the original's "negro" as a race-marker, for in 1920, it was a far less scandalous and improper appellation than it's become to our politically correct eyes and ears today. Again, Vischer has all the racial stereotypes in place and at work: in the opening scene, the negro "dances, [... hearing] the jungle roar," then "grins, baring his teeth," his "twitching sex" having impregnated a white harlot (56). During Jörg's visit to "Caoutchoucstate, Africa," the locals are habitually referred to as "cannibals" (79) and in one episode they want "to tear the skin off the smug ivory man" (80). At the same time, it's to these "cannibals" that Jörg delivers lectures on subjects such as the theory of relativity and "general suffrage for women" and is described as speaking "Cannibal better than European." The Negroes, although lacking modcons like the telephone, still understand Morse code and even establish a "Club of female negroartists" (79). And, the opening scene of Jörg's imaginary birth brings home the highly provocative point (at least for 1920) of Jörg's racially mixed origin—he is born with "motley ears: the one white, the other black" (57). The voice in Jörg's embryonic head even has it that "the white [ear] is dumb like field Europe, hears nothing. The black one, however, hears everything: the bygone & to-be, till they've both come full circle" (55). As if the black race were endowed with wisdom and powers of divination to which the white race has grown deaf. Upon conquering his first Eskimo, Jörg gives vent to the following proclamation: "Here still reigns the free, primitive huge lust of procreation. Da da! Here's the mother of all culture. Where I come from, the accursed west, there's just the grin of indictable exhibition instead of culture" (72).

These and other excursions into non-European cultures and Europe's colonised other serve Vischer the obvious purpose of critiquing some of the underpinnings of European sociopolitical ideology. And, after all the chauvinist humiliation and reduction to which *Second through Brain* subjects women, comes the following passage from Jörg's presidential inauguration speech: "In the end there's no difference whatsoever between penis & vagina, the more so when they're sweetly sighingly together, both consist of flesh, although of a slightly diverse geometrical form, they smell of mystery, which just consists in friction with the ignition of knallgas" (89). Not only is the penis no different from the vagina, but ultimately, one feels that it is the male psyche's fear of, and incompetence in front of, its female other, that is caricatured and mocked through Jörg's obsessive single-mindedness, the joke ultimately on him.

And on others, as well. Most unambiguous is Vischer's critique of that which he sets out to abandon and keeps coming back to: "the plagued canopy bed Europe" and its insane power-hunger that recently (and Vischer knew this first-hand) brought the world to the brink of self-destruction. Politicians of all ranks, real or imaginary, are a constant target of satire and scorn—as the great machinists of the sort of wisdom that drowned millions in the trenches at Verdun and gassed hundreds of thousands at Ypres. This is, of course, the dark and serious undertone of most of dada programmatic inanity and irrationality—in a world whose rationality has killed millions, zany is the new wise. This undertone also runs the length of Vischer's text from the Prologue's opening nod to Carl Einstein's point regarding "the courage to say utter rubbish" (51).

An emblem of Vischer's mockery of European rationalism is the wonderful scene with Pythagoras as the Man in the Moon, insisting on the falseness of his theorem, for "all is circle, never square," square defined as "endless nonsense with negative power" (81). If this isn't ludicrous enough, Pythagoras's tidings get distorted and vulgarized into an advertising slogan at the Berlin parliament when Jörg passes on "his friendly greetings, telegrams and the offer to buy his suspenders, which he manufactures himself, brand 'Hercules'" (90). And when Jörg does finally relate the revision of Pythagoras's theorem as "there's no straight line whatsoever, there's only circle," the reception is quite unambiguous, "they laugh, they all laugh, laugh" (95). The last poignant laugh, again, is on Jörg, for his fall is no circle but a fairly straight line with some pretty definitive end.

SECOND THROUGH BRAIN "RADIANTLY SPLATTERED"
The world of 1920, Vischer's *Second through Brain* seems to insist, has turned religion into profanity, politics into opportunism, humanism into ridiculousness, and learnedness into stupidity, and its only straight line is the trajectory of life falling into death. But Vischer's text, while posing as fictional dada manifesto critiquing (and lampooning) contemporary socio-politics, also presents a theory-in-practice of art. Most obviously, Vischer's protagonist is an artist in his own right, even though his is a practical art—stuccoing, halfway between masonry and painting/sculpting. On his downward trajectory, he does dabble in various trades and practical arts (bricklaying, carving, engraving, etc.), before finally reverting to his original calling of a stuccoist, his self-consciousness having undergone something of a sea-change in between: "I'm an artist!… I've learnt something, I can something, I am something, even when imaginarily. For suddenly he was a stuccoist. But then again he'd once been told he's more than that, he's an artist" (95).

The question of what constitutes art and what makes those engaged in the activity into artists, is of course crucial for the WWI generation of avant-gardists, and for dada in particular. Curiously, apart from a Nietzsche quote, Vischer chose for the motto of his text a self-quotation from a passage of Jörg's transformation back into the falling stuccoist: "Art is, if not already a prejudice, then still always a private view," such is the "dubious thought" (96) flashing through Jörg's brain as it is about to bespatter the pavement. This insistence on the private, anti-public or communal aspect of art chimes well with what later theorists of the avant-garde like Peter Bürger came to regard as a defining trait of Dadaism: "Dada, the most radical movement within the European avant-garde no longer criticises the individual aesthetic fashions and schools that preceded it, but criticises art as an institution:

in other words with the historical avant-garde art enters the stage of 'self-criticism.'"[24] Apart from self-quotation and self-parody, there is also self-representation, as Vischer himself is mentioned in *Second through Brain*, and argument is put forth (just as Jörg is sworn in as president) that Dadaism and Dadaists be exempt from paying taxes, "for surely Melchior Vischer's dada-games are the most inexpensive we've got at the moment" (90). The darker point of this satirical barb concerns the permissibility, the acceptance of Dadaism by powers-that-be: what is the point of launching an aesthetic revolution if it fails to affect the political status quo?

There are three further critical points Vischer's text seems to be making vis-à-vis the 1920 situation of fiction and art. The first one's to do with its academic underpinnings, subjected to systematic buffoonery, as when, at a restaurant, Jörg is served "good Pomeranian geese," all of which have "PhDs in German studies, write lyrical poetry, diaries, drama too" (88). That the alternative value-determining force, the literary market, has very little charm for Vischer, is brought home by his satirising of such popular literati of his times as "HCM" and "otto-ernst", who happens to be present at the pub table, "wondrously naked, only behind him a gorgeous bunch of flowers stuck in his honoured buttocks" (88).

The second point concerns the "art" of advertising. Vischer the newspaperman populates his text with a plethora of commercial slogans and catchphrases, knowing full well that the newspaper is the medium concentrating the most innovative potential within the print culture of his time. The very segmentation of his book into brief, usually single-paragraph instalments, and the non-linear, episodic and fragmented story told through them, both clearly point to a journalistic sensibility at work. Ironically, Vischer's only typographical experimentation, apart from the occasional non-lexical onomatopoeia, springs from his inclusion of advertisements into the text—it is, after all, "a noticeboard aglow with golden letters" advertising "eggs and buttershop" (98), that is the last thing flashing through Jörg's brain. A critique bringing into relief the banalisation, through the brevity and flashiness of the advert, of public discourse, resounds most prominently in the Pythagoras episode, where the refutation of his theorem is presented through nonsensical commercial jingles ("Odol

---

[24] Peter Bürger, *Theory of the Avant-Garde*, trans. Michael Shaw, with foreword by Jochen Schulte-Sasse (Minneapolis: University of Minnesota Press, 1984) 22.

cleans the teeth, indeed" [95]) and Pythagoras' defense is undertaken via an "advertisement banner": "Do not laugh, Your Lordships, for you don't know if it's yourselves you're laughing at. But then it's I who laugh. Who can tell you a square always and everywhere remains a square. Laugh you all, laugh!" (95)

Apart from the newspaper, the speed and disconnect of Vischer's "freakily high-torqued" narrative also strongly resounds with its third art-related topic, the cinema; its ride in a Milky-Way cab reminiscent of the 24-frame-per-second pace of the moving pictures, and, together with it, symptomatic of the acceleration of all things off-screen to which film contributes. "Off to a brothel, then!," commands Jörg, and on the next line, he's already there, with an impersonal voiceover beckoning: "Come Jörg, watch how you're being made, it stank drunken, how black and white reeled in the small divanadorned chamber, and the woman sighing rubbed herself against the musclehard loins of the Moorish athlete, what an enigma wheezing off" (55). The copulation between the negro and the prostitute is described with abstract visual economy of "black and white reel[ing]." There is the audio "sighing" and "wheezing," even some olfaction ("it stank drunken"), but the primary sense, as ever so often, is the sight of the voyeuristic proclivity ("come watch"). Again, cinema is elevated and imaginatively reconceived (e.g. "Suddenly a crank somewhere in my braincinema gyrated" [95]), but also satirised as a trivialising, lowly art form; as when Jörg celebrates New Year's Eve by "a Henny Porten screen" (68), or when the narrator satisfies the need to provide a second, more final ending to the tale, "for the sentimental, everything-ought-to-have-an-end folks with tearjerked, possessed cinesouls out there" (100).

In a culture dominated by the frag/seg/mented typography of the newspaper and the visual mode of the cinema, where the fiction's been partitioned between academics and the marketplace catering to the reading masses, the question to be posed is, how is literature to continue playing a role of any importance? Vischer's answer in *Second through Brain* is, only by taking stock of contemporary advances in other media and art forms, in accelerating its stories to the breakneck pace of the times. The first necessary step toward doing so is, of course, to adjust its language.

"HEAR THE WORD"

Of course, *Second through Brain* is much less an interesting story or a dada manifesto/programme than it is a linguistic experiment, an attempt at making language, together with the narrative, to "torque freakily high." It is a text that forges its own peculiar idiom, lexically and morphologically, as well as grammatically and syntactically. All these levels can be seen at work in the following, more than less randomly chosen passage:

> Giddy at the odour of his sweat, nearly snorted her head off, panted, drank, bit. By day she held him hidden in a small room. No longer savouring her body, her cravings, he sprang up, whacked jingling through the window, fell sorely onto the cross, already up, over the park masonry in a swing, ran upcountry. Fruits wrenched from trees, nourishment to him. Through dust, which whitely poured through all the winds, past cloisters, avoiding sbirri, who were, capped in scarlet red, searching the army streets looking for him, finally at sunsink he entered the noisy broadthroughstreeted city. He threw into a hawker's oafish face question after the name of the place: Milano. (62)

The dramatic, rhythmical, concentrated language-effect comes about by Vischer's utilisation of the four principal means: syntactically short units focussed on verbal phrases ("no longer savouring… he sprang…whacked jingling… fell… ran"); elisions of grammatical words like prepositions (there're no "ands" to mark the last members of series) or auxiliaries ("got already up"; "fruits wrenched from trees were nourishment to him"); and morphological and lexical neologisms based on portmanteau agglutination ("sunsink"; "broadthroughstreeted"). This proclivity for portmanteau compression affects not only Vischer's nouns or adjectives, but also adverbs—reading on within the same paragraph, Jörg sleeps "morningtill" and later on treads "Alpsward." This goes hand in hand with Vischer's emblematic—since already entailed in the book's title—tendency to omit articles, both definite and indefinite (not "Eine Sekunde durch das Hirn," and consequently not "*A* Second through *the* Brain").

All this, to which add Vischer's predilection for archaisms, slang, phonetic misspellings, and various jargons, gives the passage (and the entire text) an air of intensity and economy, if also unsettling evasiveness. Some of Vischer's portmanteaux are flashy, if rather forced, puns, of which some are translatable straightforwardly (as when "hyena" and "hygiene" combine in order to form "hyegienic" [93]), some less so ("bedauert" / "betrauert" approximated as "bemourned" / "bemoaned" [63]). Some are rather innocent-looking, and untranslatable, as in the remark regarding Jörg's black ear, "es hört so genau, daß es weiß"—with the delightful double entendre on "knowing" and "whiteness." Our translation can only approximate this by the more forced "it hears so exactly it's sharp-whited" (55). Regarding Vischer's experimentation with/against articles and noun-determination, a brief note on the translation here will be necessary since there're differences between the morphological makeups of German and English that allow the economy of his style to get across only to some extent. In the above passage, for instance, the original's "landeinwärts lief" is faithfully reproduced as "ran upcountry" and "warf er [...] Frage," as "he threw [...] question"—i.e. without the "correct" article.

However, German adjectival declination allows adjectives to stand-in for articles as case-determiners (e.g. Vischer has "in kleinem Zimmer" instead of the more usual "in einem kleinen Zimmer"), which has no analogue in English, and having "in small room" would not only sound faulty, but also take Vischer's experiment a step further than he himself ventured, producing a translation of a defamiliarisation more alien than the original's. The translators have tried to make up for this "wordiness" by making as much use as possible of abbreviated forms of auxiliaries and of ampersand in lieu of the usual coordinative conjunction—at least approximating the sense of deviation from the norm of the "literary" English of 1920 produced by Vischer's compression of gender and declination markers in his German.

"A PRETTY FALL, A FINE FALL"

The completion of this translation (October 2015) almost overlapped with the centenary of the founding of the Zürich Cabaret Voltaire and, together with it, dada as such. An anniversary this momentous leads one ought to raise the question of how useful, after a hundred years have elapsed, a translation can be in the case of a book so much of its own day and age, by an author that the past century seems to have done perfectly well without, in fact would rather keep in near-complete oblivion. Now, in 2017, as in 1920, time again seems to be "molluscan," but to bemoan that "inanity" passes off for "apodictic wisdom," that to be "daft" is so often to be considered "clever," is to commit a banal cliché; boundaries between the "made-up" and the "true"—if they ever were there—have in any case long ceased to exist. Only what used to be avant-garde shock tactics and reserved for special occasions is now called TV News Show and happens on a daily, hourly, minutely, secondly basis. But for a time again so similar, *Second through Brain*'s journey across this planet and off to the Moon and the Milky Way, as well as Vischer's own journey from F to V and back again, from dada to Nazi pop to West/East Berlin and to the great beyond, perhaps offer a few potentially useful reminders.

The text reminds us that only such aesthetic programme is revolutionary that seeks (to paraphrase Marx) not only to describe its own present condition and medium, but to change them. That mere parody and caricature—with economic gains in mind moreover—can never bring about a change in and of themselves. That fiction, if it is to keep pace with the general acceleration of civilisation, has a lot of catching up to do. That fiction immersed in opportunism and commercialism need not be opportunist and commercial itself. The author reminds us that radical artistic tendencies do not easily translate into radical socio-political positions; that they can actually flip into their opposite when geared up to organised political praxis; that "molluscan" times breed "molluscan" characters.

In 1918, not only did Fischer the pacifist soldier change into Vischer the radical poet, but Fischer the Sudeten-German was turned into the citizen of the artificial pan-Slavonic anti-German league called Czechoslovakia. His rather one-sided attempt at aligning himself with international avant-garde can be seen as a logical step toward overcoming his WWI traumas by creating an international network (stretching out from Prague via Berlin, Hannover and Zürich to Paris) of creative brains within which to weather whichever future storm may be in store. How this project was to be frittered away, and why V/ Fischer the Sudeten-German was to founder together with it, would be a subject for a whole other essay—any attempt to read the Emil Fischer of 1940 back into the Melchior Vischer of 1920 should be avoided.

Whether or not these reminders are in any practical way useful today, or can only be revisited as atavisms, as fossils from an age so ancient it is incomprehensible to us (just as the Christian crosses the text evokes throughout), it is this essay's firm belief that Vischer's

Second through Brain deserves at least a chance at a Second Coming, since the second it portrays speaks not only of its own time, but also anticipates much of the following century and our own time, and the brain it passes through—even a hundred years after it "spritzed on the asphalt, broke forth into yolk, mixed-in slimily with the muck, & expired" (98)—is still well worth an attempt at resuscitating.

David Bromige
will not be reading

Ken Edwards

Who was David Bromige? I recall meeting him in the 1980s on his
visit to Britain, where he was born in 1933. He had emigrated to
Canada as a fledgling, and from the early 1960s lived and worked in
Northern California. Now he was scheduled to read at the Subvoicive
poetry reading series in the upper room of a London pub. Given
the floor, he stood up to make an announcement: David Bromige
sadly could not make it after all, but he, whoever he was (for he did
not introduce himself), would read some of his work. At that very
instance, a well-known poet of my acquaintance who had been
looking forward to the reading arrived in the room, and, hearing this
and taking this person at his word, turned round and went home
disappointed (as she later confessed).

David's subterfuge – perhaps prompted by embarrassed
self-consciousness on returning to the land of his birth – clearly
backfired in this instance, but it was of a piece with his generally
sceptical approach to matters of authorship and authenticity. Not
to mention intention. In an interview with Tom Beckett in the David
Bromige issue of *The Difficulties* (1987), trying to deflect questions
about "song" and by implication the lyric voice, he states "I am
interested in a present writing, and find the pretext of presence

counter-productive." And later in the same interview: "Exaggerating this point for clarity's sake, I'd say that DB is only an accidental appendage of the poetry I've published, knowing less about it in thinking to know more, and that we need to keep in mind the image of the poet as a bus, its destination printed on its forehead, unviewable from its window-eyes."

Nevertheless, there was a real person called David Bromige, and he was a delight to be with, as many will attest. I met him for a second or third time when I was staying briefly in San Francisco in 1994, and Kathleen Fraser, a friend and fan of his, kindly offered to drive me to Sonoma County. David had booked me in for the reading series he ran at the Johnny Otis Café, Sebastopol, not far from where he and Cecelia and their young daughter Margaret were living with a number of cats and a rabbit. In the garden, David had begun fashioning an incipient maze of morning glory. Kathleen had the idea of reconstructing a conversation on a train that she had had in England with me, Susan Gevirtz and the English poet John Seed, but as I could remember almost nothing of the original conversation, and as Susan, who had come for the reading, needed to return to San Francisco, and furthermore, as David would have to stand in for the absent John Seed, it didn't really work as a reconstruction. However, a 90-minute cassette tape was made of a three-way conversation, and if it still exists it is my impression that something of interest may be on it.

The reading the previous night was an occasion I greatly enjoyed. The other reader was a very good American poet, Gillian Conoley. Also enthusiastically present was Cydney Chadwick, then editor of *Avec*, a friend of David's and a fine writer I've lost contact with. As an academic teacher (he had just taken early retirement from Sonoma State University), one might have expected David to curate a reading series at college, but instead this was like a series of jazz nights at a supper-club. People actually eating meals and drinking while listening to mostly avant-garde poetry. There were about thirty there that night, sitting at tables. And they did seem to listen. My only regret was not meeting the legendary Johnny Otis himself.

Yes, conversation with David was a delight. The following day he drove me out to Bodega Bay, the setting of *The Birds*, where we conversed over an Anchor Steam beer in a bar where we could observe sea-lions in the water outside and, sitting on railings, fat juvenile herring gulls which may have had malicious intent. He spoke nostalgically about cricket, and about following English football (soccer) on cable television – "...and I don't mean just Manchester United or Liverpool but West Bromwich Albion and Stoke City," he explained. His voice sounded Canadian to me, but he told me Americans thought he had an English accent, and he had in fact exploited this by doing voiceovers for commercials: a possible career opportunity for me, he suggested, should I ever emigrate to the US. We talked about the challenges of writing prose fiction; he disagreed with the snooty disdain I then had for dialogue, arguing there was nothing wrong with it, and besides "it usefully uses up a lot of space" – his approach to writing being nothing if not pragmatic.

So poetry is not dialogue, and the author is not the poem's protagonist, but then again.... One can't help but hear the sound of his discourse come alive again in the apparently endless flow of "Waiting For Anyone But Godot", for example – first shown in that 1987 issue of *The Difficulties*, as it happens. Actually an endless flow of jump cuts. Where is this going? The poet doesn't know, or if he does, he's not going to tell you. I am reminded of the similar endless flow of Ashbery, but the sensibility is slightly different; there isn't the mystery of a missing interiority, it's much more on the surface, more cynical, more ironic, mischievous if you like, but at any rate always practical: "...Time / to put on the water for / morning tea, I recalled, / so did, and then / had to think of something / to do that wouldn't / take very long as the water / boils almost at once / in the small saucepan. / To resume the novel found / so hilarious last night / might be to burn / the bottom out. / So I watched a segment / of "Sesame Street" / standing up."

I am reminded of:

VLADIMIR: That passed the time.
ESTRAGON: It would have passed in any case.
VLADIMIR: Yes, but not so rapidly.

The poem seems indeed to be about passing time, its considerable wit carrying the reader through the various paradoxes and sometimes felicities entailed by, for example, the notion of intention: "On Thursday / we intend to drive / over the mountains / to the hot springs / and this is attractive / both due to the destination / and the deep / satisfaction obtained / from an intention / realized." There is some cod-psychological back-story: "...More / personally, as a child / I endured considerable / anguish — my mother / hated to make / plans and my father / made meticulous / itineraries which / created great / anxiety in him, now / responsible for their / execution under the / withering eye of his wife." But whether this is an accurate picture of the childhood of DB, and whether it in any sense elucidates the poem cannot be determined.

The jump cuts take us onward effortlessly anyway: a passage devoted apparently to brief summaries of the plots of perhaps imaginary or at least unlikely movies, before veering elsewhere at mention of the word "gold": "Stern railroad / superintendent reveals / his heart of gold. / The dollar / being strong / that summer, we / would have been dumb / indeed not to avail / ourselves of it." The poem wanders into areas of mythology and mythologising and representation and art, then wanders out again, ending with the ironic/iconic image of the Sunday paper landing on the lawn with a TV guide inside – for this is of course merely one episode in the sequence "American Testament".

At this stage of his poetic career, David was close to some of the Language writers, and we can detect the influence here, for example, in the attention to surface and multiplicities of reference, of the "new sentence" of Ron Silliman or Lyn Hejinian, albeit the sentences are here chopped into verse – but of course the influence is decidedly mutual. David was one of those forebears, also including Barbara Guest, Jackson Mac Low, Robert Grenier and others, whom the Language writers claimed for their own while remaining *sui generis.*

There was talk of David having a Reality Street book out, but it didn't happen. Later on – and it was after the distress of seeing him in a wheelchair ten years later at CCCP, Cambridge, England, where he nevertheless read with his customary wit and brio – I discussed the possibility of Reality Street bringing out his Collected Poems. In 2009, before any more progress could be made on that, he died. Ron Silliman, with the help of Bob Perelman, worked long and hard on putting together the very considerable oeuvre, and it eventually became evident that the project, now monumental in every sense of the word, was unmanageable and unfeasible for my press. So it was a considerable relief to me that New Star Books of Vancouver, where David had begun his academic life, were persuaded to take it on. I look forward to that volume, but it will be no adequate substitute for his presence. If you wanted time to pass rapidly and pleasurably, no matter how awful the prevailing political climate night be – and not ignoring that climate, but cocking a snook at it – well, David Bromige was your man.

Listening and Commemoration: Maurice Scully

Nerys Williams

The books are not 'collections' of disparate 'poems', but pieces, tesserae, that make-up a larger shifting picture or thought–sound-world. Dip in anywhere, even the very beginning if you must, and go float. I'm not trying to be 'original' or eccentric in this; it's just the way I work, and I'm comfortable with it. Having read one piece the best thing is to go on to the next. And the next, and the next. One will throw light on the other eventually, picking up a repetition a variation a distant echo, changing the meaning of the preceding as the reading progresses and drawing a strange energy from the spaces between.[i]

Maurice Scully's poetry has been described by Billy Mills as a 'poetry of learning to live with and in the world, not explaining and improving on it'[ii]. Scully's evolving work *Things That Happen* was published in a series of four volumes as *5 Freedoms of Movement* (Devon, Etruscan Books 2002 /Originally Galloping Dog 1987); *Livelihood* (Wicklow, Wild Honey Press 2004); *Sonata* (London, Reality Street Editions, 2006); and *Tig* (Exeter, Shearsman Books, 2006). These volumes, spanning 1981-2006, mark the work of a writer at rest and reflection; the poems respond to, but never simply describe events. Scully's poetic is one of responsiveness and encounter. Some readers have commented on the evolving nature of his work, his poetics of extension and expansion. Others have stressed the phenomenological aspect of his poetry, its mobility and responsiveness to a sense of being in the world. One could also think about Scully's writing as ventilating the idealisation of the book as form, offering an expansive form of design, or an accumulative poetics. As the poet stresses in the citation above, one can dip into the sections of serial poems and be propelled to omnivorously read on. And this is what one is seduced into doing especially in the later volumes which include *Humming* (Shearsman Books 2009) and *Several Dances* (Shearsman, 2014).

These recent poems published in *Golden Handcuffs Review*, 'Pip' and 'Patch Work', are from a larger projected work entitled *The Play Book*. Other excerpts from this longer work have appeared as the chapbook *Play*, by Smithereens Press, accessible at http://www. smithereenspress.com/index.html and in the Trinity College literary journal *Icarus* www.icarusmagazine.com. I draw reference to *Play* in particular not only to stress the Scully's frequent use of seriality, but to make note of the chapbook's cover. *Play*'s cover might at first seem fairly innocuous, it depicts red, yellow. green, white and blue tiddlywinks, seemingly scattered mid-game. Tiddlywinks of course is often diminished as a child's game that one graduates from to other more adult pursuits. However, since Scully's poem 'Patch Work' also closes with a game of tiddlywinks, I became intrigued.

Tiddlywinks I discovered was far from a childish game. Tracing the etymology of the word offers an intriguing history. The word tiddlywink once referred to 'a. An unlicensed public-house or pawnshop; a small beer shop b. rhyming slang a drink'. Used figuratively, tiddlywinks denotes 'a useless or frivolous activity; *esp.* in phr. *to play tiddlywinks*, to waste time on trivia.'[iii] One plays the games with coloured counters named as 'winks' and the basic premise is to deliver one's own winks to a pot. However there is an offensive strategy to the game, one can prevent one's opponents by immobilising other's counters. Mary-Ann and Robert Dimand specifically mention tiddlywinks in the context of authority and strategy in their history of game theory: 'The application of "dominance" depends on the objective of players and the rules of the game played: this definition of solution apples to problems of individual optimization, cooperative games, games of tiddlywinks and games of politics.'[iv] The sketching of gains and losses is evident in this extract from the poem 'Placed', from Scully's chapbook *Plays:*

NERYS WILLIAMS | 225

PLACED

Plastic disk
laughs into
its cup.

The plastic
flat primary
colour of it.

The green
disk blinks
into its cup.

Don't let
the cup
tumble.

Dice tickle
the board.
Flick.

Slim textures
in circles squares
diamonds cylinders –

I heard
you rang
you answered
you

you parked
in the park
you too parked
next to the park

roof
roof-roof
roof-roof-roof

disk by disk
the cups open
uplaugh

Scully moves us through a repeated sequence of action and event. There are oppositions here between chance and strategy, between 'dice' and 'flick'. One might also hear echoes from Stéphane Mallarmé's *Un Coup de Dés Jamais N'Abolira Le Hasard* (*A Throw of the Dice will Never Abolish Chance*). Scully's interest however, is not in the typographic flourish and the concrete aspects of poetry on the page, or of writing just as materiality. Focusing on sound and sight, 'Placed' depicts the coordination between eye and body and moves from these dynamics to consider the realm of interpersonal communication. There is a shift from literal games, tiddlywinks and others (given the poem's emphasis on shapes circles, squares and diamonds) to language games, between and the 'I and you'. The poem thwarts any lazy linguistic expectations, *pay attention* it seems to tell us since even the change in a phoneme can disrupt our preconceived meaning. For example laugh becomes 'uplaugh' and associative expectations are thwarted as in the disk which blinks rather than winks (given the context of tiddlywinks). Strategies of defamiliarisation elicit humour, how a dice may 'tickle the board'. The patterning of phrases is key to this slight section from 'Placed'. Prepositions alter ideas of space 'you parked/ in the park' becomes 'you too parked/ next to the park'. This testing out of spatial relations is mirrored in the negotiation between speakers. We remain uncertain if this begins a discursive exchange: 'you rang/ you answered'. There are also suggestions that this could be the testing out of the syntax of an instruction primer. The accumulative repetition of '*roof*- eventually becomes the onomatopoeic transcription of a barking dog.

I would be reluctant to reduce Scully's poetry to being purely obsessed with indeterminacy of meaning, or fetishizing linguistic irresolution. Instead, it might be useful to think of these new poems published in *Golden Handcuffs Review* as enabling us to consider the propositions of a discursive poetry. In short, how poetic expression can be thought productively 'aslant'. From the 1970s discursivity as has often been linked to a particular model of what was referred to as the 'expressive lyric'. The critic Charles Altieri identifies the dominant model of the 1970s as the 'scenic mode', and suggests that this model of the lyric poem is firmly rooted in the extension of a romantic ideology.[v] The impetus of the work is towards an expression of an inchoate interiority and the poem in his words: 'Places a reticent, plain-speaking and self-reflective speaker within a narratively presented scene evoking a sense of loss. Then the poet tries to resolve the loss in a moment of emotional poignance, or wry acceptance, that renders the entire lyric event an evocative metaphor for some general sense of mystery about the human condition' (10). The everydayness of this form of poetic writing is referred to by Robert Pinsky as a form of 'discursive' writing. For Pinsky the discursive poem or lyric presents the poet 'talking, predicating, moving directly and as systematically and unaffectedly as he would walk from one place to another'.[vi] Central to this tendency is the articulation of the subject's feelings and desires, and a strongly marked division between subjectivity and its articulation as expression. This focus on expression is frequently evoked with reference to the speaker's voice, and a suggestion of certain 'sincerity'. Broadly speaking both these models of an 'expressive' or discursive lyric', posit the self as the primary organising principle of the work.

Scully's poems too can also be thought of as discursive, but they address the interlocutor in different ways. Instead of the 'naturalness' of movement identified by Pinsky, or the moment of retrospective accounting identified by Altieri, Scully's speaker is more deeply attuned to a process of listening, as well as speaking. Jean-Luc Nancy in his reflections on the act of listening, offers a way of thinking about the dynamic between listening and the construction of selfhood. Nancy proposes that:

> To listen is to enter that spatiality by which, *at the same time*, I am penetrated, for it opens up in me as well as around me, and from me as well as toward me: it opens me inside me as well as outside... To be listening is to be *at the same time* outside and inside, to be open *from* without and *from* within, hence from one to the other and from one in the other... In this open and above all opening presence, in acoustic spreading and expansion, listening takes place *at the same time* as the sonorous event.[vii]

Scully's poems open up the possibility of how to envisage a poetics of listening and being listened to; what it is to be responsive to others, as well as being an agent in the world. Perhaps this is most apparent it his poem 'Pip'. The title alone generates multiple impressions, 'pip' as kernel or seed, or the 'pips' of a phone. One senses from this poem a countering of T.S. Eliot's proposition that to be an artist is to 'purify the dialect of the tribe'.[viii] 'Pip' indicates that it is only in the latent spread of words, their sonic mutability and constant regeneration that the convening of a discursive community can take place. Take as example the initial questioning a search for the first very 'first word'- the genesis of language that is 'trapped slick/ head slow a / splash zone/ around a gap/ that might be/ the –.' Instead of finding stability and cohesion this 'first word', Scully offers a latent expansion of expanding concentric circles of 'that *first* ((ripple)).' 'Pip' offers us an interlocutor and an addressee; it focuses on processes of listening and intersubjective exchange, including remnants of a conversation in all its flaws, misinterpretations and errors. A voice tells of 'talking to / you noticing / something/ strange'. This shared space become a 'talking to / you listening / to what/ we're speaking.' In all of these interventions 'Pip' records a shifting momentum 'a change/ a beginning/ a to each'.

In this poem, there is a constant desire for the recognition of, and even responsibility towards the other. This interaction can be sensed in the voicing and appreciation in 'each/ noticing both passing/ the over-/ lapping regions of / preparation'. This desire for a recognition of something that exceeds the self, reminds us of an ideal of an intersubjective ethics, or at its most basis a sense of responsibility to another. One might think of Emmanuel Levinas's *Otherwise than Being* and the idea of an 'encounter' not as the epic wandering of an imperial self that seeks to appropriate the other to a form of knowledge. This meeting or summoning of responsibility in the philosopher's work is prompted dramatically as a dialogic 'face to face encounter.'[ix] The insistence on the immediacy of the encounter privileges not only spontaneity, but the necessity of a performative response to the other. Indeed the face-to-face meeting with the other is evoked as a moment of epiphany.

It is important to assert that there is an inherent optimism in 'Pip'. The poem articulates a hope that this encounter (between people, between interlocutors) could 'shift an inch/ or two/ on–/ plinth– clock–/time–a long way/ back'. The visual rendering of space around the poem and the staccato intervention of em-dashes mark a fragile vertical tower of words. By contrast there is a pleasure to be found in shared space, which closes the poem. Children are described sat in a circle 'feet touching' each naming a round object 'the sun, the moon,/ an eye'. The game chronicles a movement from nouns to 'figurative expressions' to include 'the family circle,/ togetherness'. The epiphany that is rendered in Scully's poem relies on the shaping of a single word, *osani*, which is extended to the formation of a community of players at the poem's close. Working through this word game we finally arrive at an explanation of *osani* as 'the Congolese /pygmy word/ for love'.

Scully has mentioned the influence of the Irish language upon his engagement with poetic language. Not being from a native Irish speaking background, the poet recalls the initial strangeness of being sent to an Irish language boarding school: 'I'd come home from boarding school on holiday full of a language my parents didn't understand, thinking in that language and translating as I spoke, dreaming in that language, or a jumble of both' (11). Scully reads this early encounter with Irish in school and in *Gaeltacht* culture as an empowering one: 'I remember thinking how strange and stimulating it was that simple objects and actions were known to me, in a way my parents didn't know them' (11). He adds that 'the seed of the attraction to language for me may lie there, in that early experience' (11). But when Scully moved school to Dublin he found the language associated to a to a 'vehement' nationalism. He went on to study both English and Irish at Trinity College in 1971.

J.C.C. Mays states that that one of the dilemmas for the Irish poet is that 'you need to be incorporated into the tradition to be an Irish writer on those terms, or you might as well not exist.'[x] Scully's poetry offers a challenge to readers more familiar with a tamer version of contemporary Irish lyricism. Tradition is most certainly negotiated in Scully's poetry, and strains of an Irish language bardic inheritance resonate in his work. The texture of reiteration within individual poems as well as consonantal patterns point us towards an earlier oral tradition. The opening epigraph to the pamphlet *Plays* is taken from an early bardic poem attributed to Giolla Brighde Mhac Con Midhe, dated 12-13th century:

> Gémadh bréag do bhiadh san duain,
> is bréag bhuan ar bhréig dhiombuain;
> bréag uile gidh créad an chrodh,
> bréag an duine dá ndéantar

This early Irish poem depicts, according to its translator Reverend L. McKenna 'an address to some Priest who was pretending to have brought back from Rome a condemnation of the Irish bards.'[xi] In translation, the poem places the act of writing in opposition to wealth yet in tandem with a tradition of patronage:

> Though a poem be only a fancy
> it is a lasting fancy given in return for a passing one!
> Wealth, however great, is a mere phantom
> A phantom too he for whom the poem is made. (681)

During the writing of poems in *Plays*, Scully mentions that the burdens of the 1916 centenary commemoration. Tracing the composition of 'Placed' he sees a link with gaming, power and commemoration. For him the poem began with an account of a game of tiddlywinks and led to reflections on Yeats's infamous 'terrible beauty':

> I was interested in the colours & shapes as well as the rhythms of the game. The colours & shapes led to 'motley' & that, in turn, to Yeats's 'Easter 1916'. 1916 in this year of centenary, led me to think about the complexity of commemoration. Those I think were the links that made the piece.[xii]

Turning to 'Patch Work' one can read the iterative patterning of the poem as an attempt to document history, climate change and processes of making history and art. The poem offers a constant sense of beginning again. Its space opens as a studio where we are offered a composition in *media res* 'Meanwhile/ back at the/ studio'. But there are also heavy hints at a regime that governs this making. Bureaucratic orders or instructions are given 'Tick. / Sign. Number.' Clearly this poem envisions the making of an important artefact under pressure 'Time's/ tight'. Scully pays attention to detail of orchestrated movement and interaction as each of the 20 A5 sheets are touched 'with yr right/ middle/ finger & /have them / touched/ each one/ by yr/ assistant'. Later, the intrusion of an artist 'Wearing/ a blindfold' hints at a possible historic connection. Of course the figure of justice is frequently blindfolded, but one might also think of the blindfold as a preparation of a subject for execution. Given Scully's sensitivity to issues of commemoration, one could read the poem as an evocation of the martyrs of the 1916 Easter Rising. Remnants of typography emerge as 'A hammer bangs/ & its echoes angle/ back' which could lead one to consider the processes involved in the making of the Proclamation of the Irish Republic. Such was the haste of the original's production, that the printer had to improvise with the type available. In his brief essay on commemoration, Scully has drawn attention to the seduction of public monument and appeal of collective memory. He comments in *Icarus* that 'Commemorative statues & monuments are public static moments of statement about an event or person or movement.' Persuasively he proposes that 'collective memory gathers up simplifications that serve agendas not controlled or initiated by the majority of those that "remember."' In 'Patch Work' one senses an acute discomfort to the processes of recording events, there is an instruction to 'Document/ the action'. This act of witness, or recording is then allied to narcissistic 'processes that are/ self-augmenting'. Scully in his deconstruction of historical narrative, warns us of what Charles Olson referred to as the 'lyrical interference of the individual as ego'. In this case, the temptation is to turn trauma and historical event into a magnum opus, or as Scully states in 'Patch Work' – 'Opus II' and 'Opus III'.

In a recent email, Scully offered that his latest poems could be read as being part of a 'patterned work.' He adds that 'Medieval Irish bardic poetry in the shadowy background. But not (I hope) in too heavy-handed a way. Like the bardic stuff it is preoccupied with power.'[xiii] Using patterns of repetition and anaphora 'Patch Work' threads throughout variations of a statement from what reads as a newspaper or journal article on climate change.[xiv] Initially the statement reads 'apparently our/ climate's much more/ sensitive to/ small forces/ than had/ previously been/ imagined'. But during the poem displacements and intrusions extend and expand the phrase to other variations: 'converting / slight ripples/ times/ temperatures' and 'small/ forces' is adapted to 'minute forces'. The insistent repetition of the scientific assertion in its various forms and tenors, offers a desperate attempt to communicate a threat, which is either ignored or fails to elicit responsive action. The poem halts accordingly with the aphoristic statement 'Ars longa/ vita brevis/ So.' The actions of reading and responding to pages close with a rapt observation of a game of tiddlywinks. Placed as a conclusion to a treatise on climate change, the gaming may initially appear inconsequential– fiddling while Rome burns. We are though reminded that the tactic of tiddlywinks is to assert dominance and be a winner- 'you win' is the poem's hollow assertion at the close. Playing or gaming, in Scully's recent poems are often provocative acts and in this last poem, become acts of aggression and power. Through Scully's forensic attention to rhythmic patterns, intrusions and pauses he creates poems that pay attention to the linguistic games that we play. Scully's poems in *Golden Handcuffs Review* perform acts of listening, while deconstructing ideas of witness and commemoration, offering an important praxis to how we might review the discursive in contemporary poetry.

.

[i] Maurice Scully, 'Interview with Maurice Scully by Marthine Satris' *Contemporary Literature* 53.1 (2012): 1-30 (p. 13)

[ii] Billy Mills, 'Sustainable Poetry' *Elliptical Movements* Accessed: https://ellipticalmovements.wordpress.com/tag/maurice-scully/

[iii] *Oxford English Dictionary* Online Accessed: http://www.oed.com.ucd.idm.oclc.org

[iv] Mary-Ann Dimand, Robert W. Dimand *The History Of Game Theory, Volume 1: From the Beginnings to 1945* (London: Routledge, 2002).

[v] Charles Altieri, *Self and Sensibility in Contemporary American Poetry* (Cambridge: Cambridge University Press, 1984), p. 10.

[vi] Robert Pinsky, *The Situation of Poetry* (Princeton: Princeton University Press, 1976), p. 133.

[vii] Jean Luc-Nancy, *Listening* translated Charlotte Mandell (New York: Fordham University Press, 2002) p. 14.

[viii] T. S. Eliot, 'Little Gidding', *The Four Quartets,* in *T.S. Eliot: Collected Poems* (London: Faber & Faber, 1970) p. 205.

[ix] Emmanuel Levinas *Otherwise Than Being, or, Beyond Essence* trans. Alphonso Lingis (Heidelberg: Springer, 1981).

[x] J.C.C Mays 'Flourishing and Foul: Ideology, Six Poets and the Irish Building Industry *The Irish Review* 8 (1990): 6-11

[xi] L. McKenna 'A Bardic Poem' *The Irish Monthly* 47. 558 (Dec 1919): 679-82 (p. 679).

[xii] Scully, 'For Icarus' *Icarus* 67.1 http://www.icarusmagazine.com/winter-2016/

[xiii] Scully, personal email 11th July, 2017.

[xiv] Scully's phrasing and rephrasing in the poem reads as a variation on headlines reporting the findings from the research article by Tobias Friedrich, Axel Timmerman, Michelle Tigchelaar 'Eocene atmospheric CO_2 from the nahcolite proxy' *Geology* 43:12 (2015)

Cavalcanty by Peter Hughes (Carcanet Press): Medieval on a scooter

Ian Brinton

In a letter from late 1831 to Julius Charles Hare of the Philological Museum William Wordsworth made a comment concerning his experiments in translation:

> Having been displeased, in modern translations, with the additions of incongruous matter, I began to translate with a resolve to keep clear of that fault, by adding nothing; but I became convinced that a spirited translation can scarcely be accomplished in the English language without admitting a principle of compensation.

The translation work that Wordsworth was engaged with was from Virgil's *Aeneid* and one poet laureate was commenting upon another when C. Day Lewis referred to this passage in his 1969 Jackson Knight Memorial Lecture on 'Translating Poetry':

> By this principle we presumably mean putting things in which are not there, to compensate for leaving things out which cannot be adequately rendered.

Day Lewis went on to suggest that much greater liberties can justifiably be taken with lyric verse than with narrative or didactic and that very word *liberties* possesses a hint of danger, revolution, of turning a world upside down: taking a liberty! In translating Cavalcanti's 'Canzone' (*Donna mi priegha*) Ezra Pound had suggested that the poem, "may have appeared about as soothing to the Florentine of A.D. 1290 as conversation about Tom Paine, Marx, Lenin and Bucharin would to-day in a Methodist bankers' board meeting in Memphis, Tenn." Pound showed his translation of 'Canzone' to Ford Madox Ford and twenty-six years later, in the Preface to his own collected poems, Ford suggested that aureate diction was a civic menace because the "business of poetry is not sentimentalism so much as the putting of certain realities in certain aspects." He went on to say that poetry like everything else, in order to be valid and valuable, must reflect the circumstances and psychology of its own day: "Otherwise it can be nothing but a pastiche."

Cavalcanty by Peter Hughes arrives with no sentimentalism and its up-to-date lack of compromise is announced on the cover of the Carcanet publication as we are confronted by a late-Medieval figure on a scooter with bubble-gum bursting from his mouth. This Cavalcanti is presented to us as a lover who recognises the age in which he lives and we see the sonnet '*Un amaroso sguardo spiritale*' as a love poem placed firmly in an estuary suburban twilight:

> I'm buoyed by her enthusiastic glance
> in my direction that was actually
> aimed at something random far behind me
> so I'm surging towards nothing once again
> tail wagging lips whistling throwing caution
> & perspective to the customary
> winds of change which flick grit & hopelessness
> into my own impercipient eyes
> while carrying any local music
> away from zones of habitation
> far out over these seductive marshes
> where the lights of doggers & illusions
> mingle with the mist & strange reflections
> will guide me down the tracks to closing time

The perky response to thinking that he is being given the eye by a girl is caught with the pun on "buoyed" but the moment of inflated ego is punctured by the realisation that she is actually looking at something/someone far behind him. The image of a dog, eagerly wanting its master, tail wagging and attendant upon the whistle, moves bleakly to the hopeless isolation of furtive sexual encounters, or illusions of them, mingling with the marsh mists. The poet's steps take the tracks back to the pub for last orders and the "closing time" rings an echo of Eliot's *The Waste Land* where the landlord calls out "HURRY UP PLEASE ITS TIME".

These translations would I think stop that Methodist Banker's Board Meeting in its tracks but they would most certainly get Ford's immediate approval.

Ed. Note: Please see the advert on the last page of this issue to understand the reference in Ian Brinton's title.

Jonathan Williams, "our Johnny Appleseed"

re. *The Lord of Orchards*, edited by Jeffery Beam and Richard Owens, Prospecta Press, Sept. 2017

Ian Brinton

On Friday 14th March 2008 Michael Rumaker, former Black Mountain College student, wrote to Jonathan Williams. Referring to him as a "fellow Piscean", poet, dreamer and visionary, Rumaker put on record his respect for the "old fellow Black Mountaineer – old Black Mountain ear – " who had spent a lifetime "keeping the word alive and sprightly in all its authentic nooks and crannies, in all the equally authentic overlooked spirits hidden in plain sight throughout the piedmont and hills of North Carolina, throughout the Southland and wherever your feet and that old station wagon took you roaming and looking."

    The Lord of Orchards is a new collection of essays and reminiscences, a reflective glance over some four-hundred and fifty pages, examining the enormous legacy left by Jonathan Williams's work. Edited with sensitive care and an accurate eye by Jeffery Beam and Richard Owens *The Lord of Orchards* is a work of fidelity and loyalty to the poet's life-work as a writer, a photographer and the founder of Jargon Press. It points us in the direction of the unique value of the man whose Stuttgart edition of the first *Maximus* poems was published as Jargon 7 in 1953 and whose conversations with Basil Bunting (*Descant on Rawthey's Madrigal*) appeared from

Gnomon Press fifteen years later. It reveals to us what Thomas Meyer wrote for *Jacket* 38 in 2009 about Williams's "panoply of detail and experience":

> His attention when it focuses centers. There is no background, foreground, or middleground. There is only what is there – a kind of "in your face" phenomenology.

Meyer had edited a *Selected Essays* of Jonathan Williams for North Point Press in 1982 and that contained the 1980 / 1981 piece written between Highlands in North Carolina and Dentdale in Cumbria, illustrating the trans-Atlantic sense of the writer being at home in two very different environments, 'The Camera Non-Obscura':

> Poets and photographers do not necessarily believe in public audiences or constituencies. They believe in *persons*, with affection for what they see and hear. They believe in that despised, un-contemporary emotion: *tenderness*.

The focussed attention of Williams's eye is caught, still, for the moment:

> From this desk in the library at Corn Close I regularly look out across the valley of the river Dee to a cluster of Scotch pines in a field of grass. The light in Dentdale, Cumbria, is unusually dim and the pines are inconspicuous and unremarkable. But, let the late sun shine its rays up the dale – particularly in a month like October – and the trees become transfigured, with the forms of the foliage and the trunks and those of the elongated shadows endlessly fascinating to the eye. The air is as cool and palpable as amber. Everything is seen 'in a new light'.

In *The Lord of Orchards* Anne Midgette's recollection is titled 'On With It' and she refers to the manner in which Williams collected things in the way that he also collected words:

> He approached the world with the attitude that there were many great things in it that not enough people knew about,

and set about finding them with a tenacity that earned him
the epithet, from Hugh Kenner, "the truffle hound of poetry."

She suggests that some of his poems have the quality of "a beach
found pebble, smooth and solid and reassuring in the palm of one's
hand" and goes on to illustrate this by quoting 'At Brigflatts Burial
Ground' written by Williams after Basil Bunting's death and then
published in *Dementations on Shank's Mare*, Truck Press 1988:

> Dear Basil,
> Eighteen months after you left us,
> poetry (that abused & discredited substance;
> that refuge of untalented snobs, yobs, and bores)
> sinks nearer the bottom of the whirling world.
>
> For the rest, you there in the earth
> hear the crunch of small bones
> as owl and mouse, priest and weasel,
> stone and cardoon, oceans and gentlemen
> get on with it...

The subtitle for the small Truck Press publication was *Being 'Meta-
Fours in Plus-Fours' and a Few 'Foundlings' Collected From
Rambles (And Drives) In Herefordshire, Gwent, Powys, Avon,
Dorset, Gloucestershire, Cumbria and North Yorkshire By J.
Williams, Gent.* It has the eighteenth-century ring of a travel guide
and contains, mostly (!), the poet's fascination with his self-styled
"dotty invention, the meta-four" the only guiding principle of which is
that each line must contain four words. Williams's humour is clear for
all to see on the opening page, 'A NOTE':

> The result (when it works) turns sense into nonsense and
> gets the mind so off-stride that you don't know whether
> you're coming or going. And you don't distinguish 'prose'
> from 'poetry'.

The quietly moving words about Bunting's grave at Brigflatts is an
exception to the four-word line and was written as if to challenge
those "untalented snobs, yobs, and bores" who might be officers of

the Poetry Police.

David Annwn's contribution to this glorious festschrift, an essay titled 'Mustard & Evening Primrose – The Astringent Extravagance of Jonathan Williams' Metafours', points us to Gustaf Sobin's work and his comments upon 'Luminous Debris'. Williams's metafours remind Annwn of Sobin's reference to Olson:

> Or Olson's interpretation of the poem as a 'high energy construct'…These indeed are archaic canons…Within that vision, the world…erupts continuously out of an irrepressible point of origin. An iridescent chaos, as Cézanne once put it…

In the 1971 Cape Goliard Press selection of Williams's poems he writes a final funerary ode to Olson which opens with the clarity of recall:

> Charles Olson made a vigorous effort long ago to teach me two things. One, that *poetry is a process, not a memoir.* Two, that there are many other uses for words than to bring the private soul to the public wailing wall.

The Lord of Orchards is divided into four different sections, 'Remembering', 'Responding', 'Reviewing' and 'Recollecting' echoing the way in which *Paideuma* was divided into 'Dove Sta Memora', 'The Periplum', 'The Gallery', 'The Explicator. There is something appropriate about this since not only was Hugh Kenner a Senior Editor of the American Journal which was devoted to Ezra Pound Scholarship but also in that individual issues were devoted to major literary figures such as George Oppen and Louis Zukofsky. In the 1980 issue, (Volume 9, Number 1) which celebrated Basil Bunting's eightieth birthday Jonathan Williams provided a set of photographs of the river at Brigflatts, the Rawthey, and wrote an uncompromising opening paragraph to introduce his contribution of eighty short questions he wanted to put to the poet:

> When a man reaches fourscore, it is assumed that he has outlived Wisdom; or is given to the curse of Old-Fartism; or has forgotten most of what he remembers. Since Basil

> Bunting does not set up as a sage and since he has made
> himself very clear on the subject of Literary Criticism (i.e.,
> there is no bloody excuse for the stuff), what is one to do
> with him on the page, with the subject here at Corn Close for
> a visit and more or less obliged to follow my literary whims?

With typical humour he titled this contribution 'Eighty of the
Best'! Despite quoting Bunting's view of literary criticism I think
that Williams would have been very pleased with the seventeen
contributions to the 'Responding' section of this new book.

The republication of Guy Davenport's essay, which had
been originally used as an introduction to *An Ear in Bartram's Tree*,
is a delight which takes us close to the central issues in Williams's
poetry:

> Jonathan Williams learned how to write a poem as trim and
> economical as a tree. And like a tree his poems have roots,
> exist against a background, and convert light into energy.
> And take their shape not only from inner design but also
> from the weather and their circumjacence.

Having been taught by Charles Olson at Black Mountain Williams
would have appreciated the accuracy of that thought. After all it was
Olson who wrote 'These Days' in January 1950:

> whatever you have to say, leave
> the roots on, let them
> dangle
>
> And the dirt
>
>> Just to make clear
>> where they come from

Ross Hair's contribution to the 'Responding' section of the
book looks closely at Williams in relation to both Black Mountain
and Olson, highlighting Williams's recognition of the energetic and
infectious nature of the man:

The most persuasive teacher I ever had was Olson...I really didn't have knowledge of or interest in the Carlos Williams / Pound line of descent. Olson opened that up for me. I found him an extremely enkindling sort of man, marvellously quick and responsive. You got a lot from him at all times.

Hair's article is no simple rewriting of literary history and he is scrupulous in his attention to the details of the way in which Jonathan Williams moved forward to discover his own voice. He quotes from Martin Duberman's *Black Mountain, An Exploration in Community*, in which in 1968 Williams points to the need to move away from Olson's influence:

> The only problem was, Olson is almost enough to wipe you out...It took me a long time to get out from under Leviathan J. Olson. Of course some poets said that I would be stuck there. They didn't like him. Zukofsky thought I was being victimized. Rexroth thought so. Dahlberg still thinks so. He asks baleful questions like "Why do you imitate Olson? and Pound?" [Dahlberg has elsewhere referred to Olson as the Stuffed Cyclops of Gloucester.] *I* don't think I do, but I would say it took me ten years to achieve whatever the thing is they call "my own voice".

Part of that discovery can perhaps be traced back to the summer of 1961 when Williams and Ronald Johnson hiked the Appalachian Trail from Springer Mountain, Georgia, to the Hudson River in New York, some 1447 miles. Williams described the trek as the "perfect training for poets: learning to attend the names of birds and plants and stars and trees and stones." This is perhaps one of the connections between Williams and Bunting who wrote to Peter Makin in 1984 that "Suckling poets should be fed on Darwin till they are filled with the elegance of things seen or heard or touched." In an unpublished letter from Bunting the poet suggests that the reader of a poem should "let the words do whatever they can with you":

> Poems are written because men are interested in putting words together, or rather in putting the sounds of words together, in such a way as to make a pattern of sound that

pleases him and might please other people.

Guy Davenport suggests that the total involvement Jonathan Williams had with the world of poetry made him "an ambassador for an enterprise that has neither center nor hierarchy but whose credentials are ancient and respected." His poetry has the "weightlessness" of "thistledown and like the thistle it bites":

> Its coherence is that of clockwork, at once obvious and admirable. Its beauty is that of the times: harsh, elegant, loud, sweet, abrupt all together. The poet in our time does what poets have always done, given a tongue to dumbness, celebrated wonderments, complained of the government, told tales, found sense where none was to be perceived, found nonsense where we thought there was sense; in short, made a world for the mind (and occasionally the body too) to inhabit.

Thomas Meyer's elegy in forty-eight threnodic pulses, 'KINTSUGI', takes its title from the Japanese practice of repairing ceramics with gold-laced lacquer to illuminate the breakage. In his brief introduction to this moving response to the dying of Jonathan Williams, Robert Kelly writes about sorrow being the true ground of language. As Geoffrey Ward put it in an article for *Archeus* (a London based magazine edited by D.S. Marriott in 1989):

> Language is doomed to unpunctuality, words chasing, describing, shadowing a reality they can do anything but actually be.

As Kelly puts it:

> It is the reference that language, in its essence and by its presumed first purpose, *makes to what is not here.* Every object or relationship or feeling, ill-roused from its sleep by words, soon slips back into lostness, pastness, leaving the same sort of aftertaste that music does.

The words that give presence to the "lostness", the "pastness", are placed on the page by Meyer as the hardest and last things to do:

> To pick up your glasses and know
> you will never look through them again.

The co-editor of *The Lord of Orchards* is Richard Owens and in a telephone interview he had with Williams on a Friday afternoon, June 1st 2007, he asked the poet about his current writing. The reply gives us a picture of a man whose poetry is not connected to any world of literary formality but whose eye is upon the *trouvailles*, those moments perceived throughout the journey:

> I do what I always do. Sit down and put words on pages and scratch around a little…I never have any agenda. That allows me space to do this and do that and not do *this*. I'm not very inclined to worry very much about theory and all that. But something goes on in some sense.

In that 'FINAL FUNERARY ODE FOR CHARLES OLSON' the humour and disdain with which Jonathan Williams treated the memoirist's world of poetry, the pompous accumulation of literary artefacts, is sheer delight:

> One knows ladies, librarians, and Hierophants of the Ego-Trip who still have pieces of the piano bench destroyed by Thomas Wolfe; the carpet be-vomited by Dylan Thomas; the glass dropped by Ferlighetti and now preserved as a mobile of slivers and silver rods; the famous Vaseline jar of A. Ginsberg; and, last but not least, the last faeces of Walt Whitman preserved in a case in the Camden Museum. At best they want the poet blind drunk, institutionalized, or suicided. *Time* has a fine list of such players.

The glasses referred to by the grieving long-term partner Thomas Meyer are not such objects and instead they are a moving reference to the windows through which the poet could see.

Michael Rumaker believed that Jonathan Williams did not read that last letter of 14th March but Tom Meyer had carried it to the hospital and had read it to the dying Williams. In an email sent to me by Rumaker on 27th March 2008 he said "I didn't realize that it would turn out to be a farewell letter – Jonathan always had such a tenacity and resilience, a toughness, really, it was impossible to believe that he wouldn't pull through this time. But nothing is guaranteed."

Notes on Contributors

Hélène Aji is Professor of American literature at the Université Paris Nanterre, Visiting Professor at the University of Texas at Austin,and President of the French Society for Modernist Studies (SEM). Recently she has edited an issue of online journal *IdeAs* on small presses and avant-garde poetry in the Americas (http://ideas.revues.org/1832, Summer 2017). At Nanterre, she co-directs the research program "Conceptualisms" on experimental American poetry and fiction, and the book series "Intercalaires."

Andrea Augé is an artist and art director for film/video living in Seattle

Ken Bolton is a Sydney poet long domiciled in Adelaide where he worked for the Experimental Art Foundation. He has published many books, edited magazines & published a good deal of art criticism. His *Selected Poems* are available from Shearsman Press.

Ian Brinton's recent publications include a *Selected Poems & Prose of John Riley* and *For the Future, a festschrift for J.H. Prynne* (both from Shearsman Books), a translation of selected poems by Philippe

Jaccottet (Oystercatcher Press) and he is working on *An Early
Prynne Reader* which is due out from Shearsman next year. He co-
edits Tears in the Fence and SNOW and is involved with the Modern
Poetry Archive at the University of Cambridge.

David Bromige, one of the truly important postwar poets, was born
in London, England in 1933. He earned degrees at the University of
British Columbia and the University of California, Berkeley. He was
Professor of English at Sonoma State University and the University
of San Francisco. He moved to Sebastopol, California, in 1970 and
died there in June, 2009.
    Bromige wrote more than thirty books, which, while mostly
poetry, also included fiction and literary theory. Notable titles
include *The Gathering* (Sumbooks Press, 1965), *Tight Corners &
What's Around Them* (Black Sparrow Press, 1974), *My Poetry* (The
Figures Press, 1980) and *Red Hats* (Tonsure Press, 1986), *The
Harbormaster of Hong Kong* (Sun & Moon Press, 1993), and *As in T,
As in Tether* (Chax Press, 2002), *The Petrarch Project* (with Richard
Denner, dpress, 2007).

Rachel Blau DuPlessis, poet, critic, collagist, is the author of the
multi-volume long poem *Drafts*, (1986-2012), from Salt Publishing
and Wesleyan, called "one of the major poetic achievements of
our time" by Ron Silliman. Post-*Drafts* books include *Interstices*
(Subpress, 2014), *Graphic Novella* (Xexoxial Editions, 2015),
Days and Works (Ahsahta, 2017), and both the collage-poem
Numbers (from Materialist Press) and *Around the Day in 80 Worlds*
(BlazeVOX), both slated for 2018. She has written a trilogy of critical
essays on gender and poetics: *The Pink Guitar, Blue Studios* and
Purple Passages, and several other critical books. She has edited
the *Selected Letters of George Oppen*, and a collective memoir,
The Oppens Remembered, coedited *The Objectivist Nexus*, and
has written on Oppen, Zukofsky and Niedecker. Also published in
2017 was *Selected Poems/Poesie scelte, 1978-2015*, translated into
Italian by Amy Ballardini.

Ken Edwards' press Reality Street is now dormant, but forty-odd
titles remain in print. He is writing every day, mostly prose, his latest
published text being *a book with no name* (Shearsman Books,

2016). A mystery novel, *The Grey Area*, has been completed but is yet to be published. He continues to live in the English coastal town of Hastings with his partner Elaine in a house full of music.

Stephen Fredman is Professor Emeritus of English, University of Notre Dame. He is the author of *Poet's Prose* (1983, 1990), *The Grounding of American Poetry* (1993), *A Menorah for Athena* (2001), and *Contextual Practice* (2010). He has edited *A Concise Companion to Twentieth-Century American Poetry* (2005) and, with Steve McCaffery, *Form, Power, and Person in Robert Creeley's Life and Work* (2010). His edition of *How Long Is the Present: Selected Talk Poems of David Antin*, was published in 2014, and a new edition of Robert Creeley's *Presences: A Text for Marisol* is due out in 2018. He is working on *Thinking Poetically*, a book of essays.

Keith Jebb has two pamphlets from Kater Murr's Press, *tonnes* and *hide white space*. In recent years poems have appeared in Veer About and Poetry Salzburg Review. He was co-organiser of the Blue Bus poetry reading series, until it ended in 2016. He is Senior Lecturer and Course Coordinator in Creative Writing at the University of Bedfordshire in Luton, England.

Hank Lazer is a proud & frequent contributor to GHR. Two new poetry books of his hand-written shape-writing are due out in late 2017 or early 2018: *Thinking in Jewish* (N20) from Lavender Ink and *Evidence of Being Here: Beginning in Havana* (N27) from Negative Capability Press. Roll Tide.

Of **Joseph McElroy's** nine novels, *Women and Men* is forthcoming in a third edition from Dzanc. He is completing a non-fiction book about water. His essay on censorship, originally a talk in Kiev, is appearing in amplified form in the United States and in Europe.

Alice Notley has published over forty books of poetry, including (most recently) *Benediction, Negativity's Kiss,* and *Certain Magical Acts*. She lives in Paris, France.

Lance Olsen's most recent books is the novel *Dreamlives of Debris* (Dzanc, 2017), a retelling of the minotaur myth. "I Spoke to Her as a

Woman : She Answered Me as a Man" is an excerpt from his novel-in-progress, *My Red Heaven*, about 1927 Berlin. He teaches at the University of Utah and serves as chair of the Board of Directors at FC2.

Peter Quartermain's memoir of English boyhood from 1939 to 1950 (the dates are fluid) is now complete. It is 16 chapters but can never be finished because, like everyone else, he gets dumber all the time. It was fun to write but enough is, after all, a lot.

Jerome Rothenberg is an internationally celebrated poet, translator, anthologist, and performer with over ninety books of poetry and twelve assemblages of traditional and avant-garde poetry such as *Technicians of the Sacred, Shaking the Pumpkin* (traditional American Indian poetry), *Exiled in the Word* (a.k.a. A Big Jewish Book), and, with Pierre Joris and Jeffrey Robinson, *Poems for the Millennium*, volumes 1-3. His most recent big books are *Eye of Witness: A Jerome Rothenberg Reader* (2013) and *Barbaric Vast & Wild: Outside & Subterranean Poetry from Origins to Present* (volume 5 of *Poems for the Millennium*, 2015). A significantly expanded fiftieth anniversary edition of *Technicians of the Sacred* has just been published by the University of California Press, and a new book of poems, *A Field on Mars: Poems 2000-2015*, was published last year in separate English and French editions.

Michael Rothenberg is editor of BigBridge.org and co-founder of 100 Thousand Poets for Change. His most recent books of poetry include *Drawing The Shade* (Dos Madres Press, 2016), *Wake Up and Dream* (MadHat Press, 2017) and a bi-lingual edition of *Indefinite Detention: A Dog Story* (Varasek Ediciones, Madrid, Spain, 2017).

Maurice Scully born Dublin 1952. Many books. Most recent *Several Dances* and *Plays* from Smithereens online press. Divides his time between Ireland and Spain.

Ben Slotky's first novel, *Red Hot Dogs, White Gravy* was published by Chiasmus in 2010 and was re-released by Widow & Orphan in 2017. His work has appeared in *Numero Cinq, The Santa Monica*

Review, Barrelhouse, McSweeney's, Hobart, Juked, and many other publications. He lives in Bloomington, IL with his wife and six sons.

Scott Thurston is a poet, mover and educator working in higher education in Manchester, UK. He has published twelve books and chapbooks of poetry, including three full-length collections with Shearsman: *Hold* (2006), *Momentum* (2008) and *Internal Rhyme* (2010). More recent work includes *Reverses Heart's Reassembly* (Veer, 2011), *Figure Detached Figure Impermanent* (Oystercatcher, 2014) and *Poems for the Dance* (Aquifer, 2017). He edited *The Salt Companion to Geraldine Monk* (2007) and in 2011, Shearsman published his collection of four long interviews with the poets Karen Mac Cormack, Jennifer Moxley, Caroline Bergvall and Andrea Brady, called *Talking Poetics*. Scott is founding co-editor of open access *Journal of British and Irish Innovative Poetry* and co-organizer of the long-running poetry reading series The Other Room in Manchester. Since 2004, he has been developing a poetics integrating dance and poetry which has seen him collaborating with dancers in Berlin and New York as well as in the UK. *Phrases* (excerpted here) is a series of poetic reflections on ongoing encounters with various dance and movement practices including Five Rhythms, Movement Medicine and Open Floor work, alongside Authentic Movement, Qi Gong and Alexander Technique. The essence of the enquiry concerns how words relate to movement and how movement can call forth language, and the consequences of this more embodied sense of self for the identity of the writer. Phrase XVIII was performed on BBC Radio 3's literary programme *The Verb* in March 2017.

David Vichnar is a critic, editor, publisher and translator living in Prague where he teaches at Charles University. His publications include *Subtexts* (2015) and *Joyce Against Theory* (2010), and a number of edited volumes. He translates into both English and Czech chiefly from German and French. His translations include Louis Armand's *Snídaně o půlnoci* (Argo, 2013) and Philippe Sollers' *H* (Equus, 2015). His co-translation, with Tim König, of Melchior Vischer's *Sekunde durch Hirn* (*Second through Brain*, 2015) is the first English translation of this iconic and yet forgotten Dada novel.

Donald Wellman is a poet and translator. He has translated books of poetry by Antonio Gamoneda, Emilio Prados, Yvan Goll, and Roberto Echavarren. *Albiach / Celan: Reading Across Languages* is from Annex Press (Spring 2017). His *Expressivity in Modern Poetry* is forthcoming (early 2018) from Fairleigh Dickinson University Press. His poetry has been described as trans-cultural and baroque. His collections of poetry include *Roman Exercises* (Talisman House, 2015), *The Cranberry Island Series* (Dos Madres, 2013), *A North Atlantic Wall* (Dos Madres, 2010), *Prolog Pages* (Ahadada, 2009), and *Fields* (Light and Dust, 1995). As editor of O.ARS, he produced a series of annual anthologies including *Coherence* (1981) and *Translations: Experiments in Reading* (1984).

Nerys Williams lectures in American Literature at University College, Dublin and is a Fulbright alumnus. She has written extensively on American (and Anglophone) poetry and poetics. Her first volume of poetry, *Sound Archive* (Seren, 2011) won the Irish 'Strong' prize in 2012 and was nominated for a Forward first volume prize. Her second volume *Cabaret* was recently published by New Dublin Press (2017).

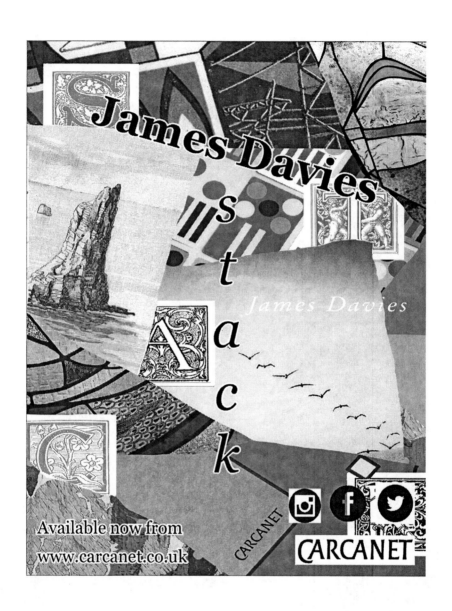

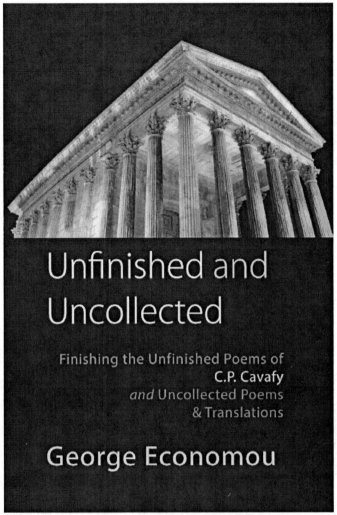

Unfinished and Uncollected

Finishing the Unfinished Poems of
C.P. Cavafy
and Uncollected Poems
& Translations

George Economou

Shearsman Books $18.00 ISBN 9781848614369

"Rather than fulfilling the conventional job of a translator, George Economou uses his poetic disposition to translate and then complete the unfinished poems of the late Greek poet C. P. Cavafy. While Economou does not insist that he is the authority on how Cavafy would have finished the poems, he presents these poems as an artistic vision, written in the spirit of a classic poet." —*World Literature Today*

"…there is really no reason why one should not use Economou's versions as his or her go-to edition of the Unfinished Poems. They keep to the spirit and more often than not the letter of the originals, and infuse with contemporary energy material that might otherwise come out flat in English. Besides, one has the added bonus of thirty-five more pages of original poetry—and ten more of diverse translations." —Martin McKinsey, *Translation Review*

Order from amazon.com or BarnesandNoble.com

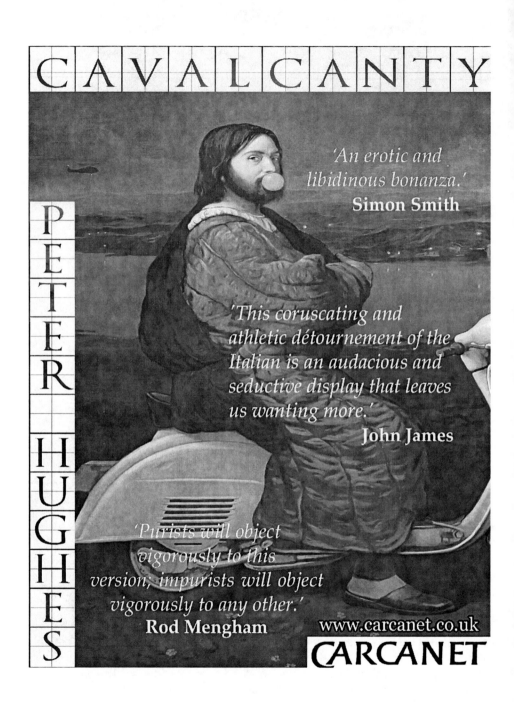

CPSIA information can be obtained
at www.ICGtesting.com
Printed in the USA
FFOW02n0755030218
44796951-44921FF